The Perfect Illusion:
Life.

John Duke Logan

Printed in the United States of America

10 9 8 7 6 5 4 3 2

Logan, John Duke., 1993—
      The Perfect Illusion: Life. / John Duke Logan. -- Massachusetts:
      2013
           p. cm.
      ISBN-10: 1479149845 (Paperback) ISBN-13: 978-1479149841 (Paperback).
           1. Magic Tricks 2. Self-Help 3. Motivation 4. Inspiration 5. Psychology 6. Philosophy 7. Games. I. Logan, John Duke. (1993–).
      II. Title.

Publication Date:
July 10th, 2013

To my parents:

Mark Fish Logan
&
Carolyn Kessinger MacDonald

For the past five years, I've been writing this book for you,
yet I kept it a secret.

Thank you for my wonderful life. Here is my gift in return.

I love you both.

Acknowledgments

Editors:

Cherie Clark, James L. Clark, Nicholas DiCienzo,
Christine Fay, John Hopkins, David Hurley, Michael
Elliott Klein, Katy Litka, Gary Mercure, Haley Nicol,
Kipp Sherry and Emily Tiedtke.

I can never thank you enough for letting me
see my potential in writing.

Closest Supporters:

Inly School, The Town of Hanover, Bryant University,
Massachusetts Youth Leadership Foundation, Tim
Brown, Tom Chiarelli, James L. Clark, David DuVal,
Christine Fay, Ronald Glennon, Sean Gold, Stephen
Hegarty, John Hopkins, David Hurley, Scott Hutchi-
son, Amanda Parry, Michael Patch, Kevin Perry,
Brett Powers, Steven Rodday, Kipp Sherry, Andrew
Stinger, Brendan Stone, Michelle Sullivan, Jim Sylvia,
Chris Taylor, Amanda Tiedtke, Emily Tiedtke, Angela
Wheeler, Gregg Wheeler, and Justin Willman.

Thank you for your continuous encourage-
ment over the years. I wouldn't be the person I
am today without you.

Photography:

Debbie Meads (DJ Meads Photography)
Emily and Daniel Tiedtke.

Thank you for creating the cover and making
things less confusing for the readers.

Family:

Claire Kessinger, John Kessinger, Angela Logan, Duke
Logan, Jacob Logan, Julia Logan, Matthew Logan,
Jason MacDonald, Sarah MacDonald,
Scott MacDonald, and MaryAnn Walsh.

Absolutely speechless.

The Opening Act

The Illusions & Tricks

The Finale

*"We are all humiliated by the sudden discovery
of a fact which has existed very comfortably and
perhaps been staring at us in private while we have
been making up our [own] world entirely without it."*

- George Eliot, *Middlemarch: A Study of Provincial Life*

The Opening Act

Introduction.

Imagine the spotlight in your face. You can feel the heat from the shine. You're on stage. It seems like a normal stage, but it's not- trust me.

You turn around and see a person behind you waiting their turn. You see a person behind him. Then another person behind her. And so on.

These strangers waiting in line are filled with their own knowledge, insight, and advice. They come from many different backgrounds, cultures, and beliefs. They are young and old. They are rich and poor. They are ambitious and content.

You realize this is it.
There is no turning back.
No second chances.
The entire human race is staring at you.
And you have one chance to say one thing.

It could be a word. It could be a sentence. It could be a paragraph. It could be anything. Anything at all.

Before you, others have spoken words of wisdom. These voices will still echo after your turn. Now is when you must decide whether or not your voice will echo as loudly, or if it will be a faint whisper that disappears quietly.

As you stand there silently for a moment on stage, your eyes gaze the crowd. You see the young and the old. You see the rich and the poor. You see the ambitious and the content.

These differences only inspire you. This inspiration helps you rearrange your thoughts as you finally realize what you will say.

You take a deep breath, reach for the microphone, and just as you're about to start speaking...

The date was October 7th, 2003 and it was my tenth birthday. As I grew older, this dream never escaped my mind. I continuously thought about what I would say in this unique situation, and by doing so, I became obsessed and fascinated with the concept of conformity, sociology, and perception. Throughout this book, I'll teach you how to combine these topics together so you can ultimately enhance your creativity and motivation, thus becoming more innovative. But most of all, don't forget about the dream you just read about. We'll get back to it later- I promise.

Perception v. Illusion

Herein lies the question we have all asked ourselves at some point or another: *what is life?* Of course there is the definition in the dictionary, but on a deeper level it's also a question philosophers have been studying since, well, the beginning of life. As a performer, here's my answer: life is an *illusion.* What do you mean? I'm glad you asked. An **illusion** is an object, event, or situation that can be perceived differently by others based on their own beliefs, despite what the reality may be. **Perception,** on the other hand, is our interpretation and awareness of a specific stimulus, in this case our interpretation of the illusion.

Even though illusions and perceptions can fall under the same category in psychological studies, they are two completely different things. For instance, *illusions* never change; it is our *perceptions* that have the ability to change. It depends on how we want to view the illusion, which impacts our overall perception (and belief) of the situation. As a result, life itself exists in such a way as to cause us to believe in different perceptions according to who we are (based on our backgrounds and experiences). Therefore, if our own individual perceptions of life vary from person to person, life in a sense is our own illusion that we constantly try to interpret by changing the way we look at it.

Perception is an interesting concept to talk about. For instance, if you were alone, closed this book, placed it down on the floor, and walked into the other room, how would you know this book would remain on the floor if you couldn't see it? In other words, does all knowledge come from perception? If this is the case, does the world we live in only consist of ideas and the minds that create and perceive those ideas? And, if this is true, does something only exist if it is perceived by others?

Exactly what are you holding right now? Honestly, it's only a little flexible rectangle filled with "words." But *your* mind perceives it as a book. And, with one glance, you're inside *my* mind. Crazy how that works, huh? Books bind people together who never knew each other; they shackle time. After reading this "book" you'll come to a conclusion that in order to see the world, we must learn to break off our familiar acceptance of it. For example, sometimes our experiences may be filled with puzzles and contradictions. When this occurs, we usually have two options: we can either put our assumptions of the world to the side or we can re-learn how to consider our experiences. Regardless, at some point, we have to disregard our approval of the world in order to perceive it from a different point of view.

Rather than writing in technical language and keeping ideas out of reach, I wrote in such a way that grounds them in everyday experiences since I perform for various age groups. For the next 155 pages, we will question the "normal" perspectives that society has "trained" us to see throughout our lifetime. This adventure we'll be going on will be chronological, starting in our childhood, moving into our adult life, and eventually meeting Death. Hopefully we can use this new knowledge to not only perform magic, but also to motivate ourselves and others, question these illusions we witness throughout our lives, and form different perceptions of these illusions. As a result, in the end, we may just figure out what our purpose in this "life" truly is.

Failure to introduce myself; that was rude of me, I apologize. My name is John Logan and I'm a performer. I guess you could say I perform "magic tricks" (and calling me a "magician" is perfectly fine), but sometimes I think the term "magician" can be too restricted for what I actually do. So *who* exactly am I and *what* exactly am I trying to prove in this book? Don't worry, I'm not going to use complicated sentences or difficult vocabulary. I tend to believe words are just symbols we can relate to: they never produce the absolute truth...about anything. So to answer your questions about who I am and what I'm trying to prove: I'll let you decide.

Each individual reading this book may judge or have a different interpretation of me as most readers normally have for the author. However, I've learned that when you're in the public eye, others will take every opportunity to criticize or praise you whether you deserve it or not. Understand that the content within these pages is only intended to support, question, or modify what you already believe. I am not here to tell you that the beliefs you hold right now are wrong in any way. I am here to show you that life can be looked at from different perspectives—for better and for worse—and I will present examples of how this can be achieved. That being said, read this book for pleasure; for enjoyment; for desire. Read this book because you want to read this book. And if you want to read this book, you have a great adventure ahead of you.

What is "Magic"?

Common stereotypes for the word "magic" probably consist of rabbits, hats, scarves, or capes. I'm not saying that is incorrect whatsoever (because, once again, that's your own perspective), but sometimes the term "magic" can be tossed around, kicked, and beaten until it becomes something that it's not. The art of magic is just a glimpse of what life could be if we stop thinking too much. This type of art proves that if we look at life from a different point of view, we can see, experience, and perform what seems like the "impossible." Sometimes it can be a depressing subject though, since not a lot of people know how to do this. As performers we tend to have a different idea of "experiencing reality."

The best part about the art of magic is that if you know how to perform magic well, the world around you will never be boring. Magic is a great tool to begin friendships, start connections, and build self-confidence. But in this book I'm not teaching you the skills you need to be a professional magician. It takes many years before one can be familiar with every aspect of the art. Throughout this book you'll start to understand what *true* magic means to me and hopefully it can change your perspective of what "magic" is as well.

The Confusing Addiction

I'll warn you now: the art of magic is addicting. Not just for you, but for the audience as well because it is the "unknown" in life that attracts us. However, people only like being deceived when it's enjoyable. If you're going to learn how to perform magic, strive to entertain rather than to trick. Though people only witness magic at a specific moment, the real impact is the resulting memory. The audience will remember that moment for a long time and that is your goal. You need to connect with the audience on an emotional level, and that is how people will remember you. Not by performing some easy card trick, but really connecting with them: magic tricks create the unexpected and the unexpected creates good stories. Eventually, you'll be performing one, two, maybe up to twenty tricks a day for strangers and friends. But here's the catch: people are curious. The only thing that keeps the audience in their seats is wondering what's going to happen next. And in order to be a successful performer you must create curiosity. As soon as you make the leap to perform magic, even if you've performed before, it changes you and how others perceive you. The art of magic is a beautiful, intoxicating, mind-altering drug.

Let me first explain to you how confusing this art can be, especially to the audience members. For instance, many people believe that there are two types of magic in this world: 1. The "real" magic and 2. The magic that performers do. The performers' magic, I guess you could call it, perfectly mimics the other type. Therefore, performers echo "real" magic, right? But, does "real" magic actually exist? And if it doesn't exist, then performers are trying to mimic, or echo, something that doesn't even exist, which is somewhat odd. Thus, "real" magic should really be considered a type of emotion or dreamlike feeling. Yet, this euphoric emotion slowly transforms into this inferior feeling that lacks knowledge. To move from something so trustworthy, yet the next moment filled mystery and confusion can be powerful, and sometimes dangerous, to the human mind. And since magic is an intellectual art, the best irony is that the more you know about the world, the more powerful magic can be to you. This art can grab us like we are puppets on strings unable to manage our own emotions for that moment. Magic can flirt with reality and inspire others at the same time. No one will ever understand how strong this art can be.

YOU Create the Memory & Experience

Learning how to do magic not only lets you share special moments with others, but it also helps you become an excellent actor. For your audience, you must always create a type of wonderland where the only things that are real are what you want them to believe.

Understanding your "style" may be difficult at first. Personally, you might never guess I perform "magic" just by my appearance. I don't wear outrageous costumes, nor do I own a black top hat. But if you're one of those people who like to dress in Harry Potter costumes and use sticks you find in your backyard as magic wands, go for it. Or if you like to be one of those magicians who can pull a hat out of a bunny, then go for it- yes, you read that right. But, no matter what, just be yourself when you perform, regardless if you have a normal appearance or not. However, in this day and age, what is "normal" anyway?

Some styles performers have correspond to the type of magic they perform. For instance, I decided to teach you "close up magic." I consider this the best type of magic because you get to witness reactions, but you also have to maintain different relationships at the same time. It's a very difficult, yet rewarding type of magic.

Why I Perform Magic

I personally have my own style, which leads to why I perform in the first place: to communicate. Once you become good at something, people start to notice you more (not just with magic, but with anything in life). Once people notice you, the opportunity to communicate becomes greater. As soon as I capture someone's attention with magic, it instantly builds a connection between us. As a result, they'll embrace my perspectives on other matters and I can embrace theirs. I have other reasons why I perform, but you'll find those throughout this book so I won't get into too much detail right now. So what exactly do I do? Well, I take the five senses and create an illusion that I have a sixth, thus impacting the perceptions people have about this world.

Perception is Everything

One example on how perception can influence our thoughts depends on what type of words are used in conversation. For instance, one might have a different vision in their head if I asked, "Did you see the two cars crash?" rather than "Did you see the two cars bump?" Even though the questions may have the same meaning, the perception may be different depending on which word was actually used ("crash" vs. "bump"). Pretty neat, huh? Another example is that the the mind usually doesn't recognize a second "the" in this sentence. Read the previous sentence again and see if you find it! In addition, the sentence "I never said she stole my money" has seven different meanings depending on which word is stressed. Examples like these prove that the performer's most valuable assistants are the minds of his or her audience members. Since the brain is such a complex tool, it's important to have the correct presentation in life since presentation impacts perception. I could probably write an entire book on that, but that's for next time. On the subject of books, how did *this* book get started? Good question.

My Story

Now some of you may be wondering how my magic "career" got started. I guess the introduction of a book is a good place to tell you.

Like many of us, when we go to family events, we tend to get bored after a few hours. Well, this happened to me. To entertain myself, I wanted to create a magic trick. After experimenting with a few ideas, I started creating my own tricks with everyday objects such as cards

The Power of Perception

Do you see a man playing the saxophone?

Or do you see a face?

Most people see an old lady.

But what happens when you turn the book upside down?

Is the glass half full or half empty?

This is a common expression used to indicate a person's perspective on a specific situation.
If the individual is an optimistic person, they would most likely say the situation is "half full." On the contrary, if the individual is a pessimistic person, they would most likely say the situation is "half empty."

These examples prove how perception can impact our thoughts dramatically. Sometimes we believe that our view is the correct (and only) way to look at a situation, but we must consider all perspectives before making assumptions. Even though your perception and opinion about something may be different from others, that doesn't mean you should disregard their point of view. Although at times you may disagree, still try to understand where they are coming from. If you value their opinion (perspective), they might value yours and this will only enhance the trust and respect within the relationship. And who wouldn't want that to happen?

and coins. A few days later I filmed myself performing some of my creations and posted a few videos online. Since I was already in the "magic-mode", I started researching more and stumbled upon a particular website that caught my eye.

I was searching through their products when I realized some were used by famous magicians such as David Copperfield, Criss Angel, and David Blaine (little did I know that the owner of the company selling the products was very good friends with David Blaine). I posted videos of my creations in their Media Section only expecting constructive criticism for what I considered as simple tricks. It was only a few minutes later when a company representative contacted me asking for my phone number. He told me just based off the videos I submitted, he was impressed with my creativity and saw great potential in me for the future. Since my face wasn't shown in the videos, he thought I was a bit older than what he expected. After numerous conversations, I signed a contract with the company becoming the youngest "creative consultant" they ever hired. Everyone else working for the company was over 25 years old while I was only 12 at the time.

From that moment on, I decided to learn more about magic. I learned the basics first and then started creating more of my own material. By performing more I became more comfortable with the art and finally understood that everything in life is based on perception. For instance, if you can question the "norm" you have the ability to enhance your creativity and motivation, thus having a more optimistic point of view in any type of situation. As the years went by, the company was intrigued by this concept and asked if I wanted to write a book about it. What you're holding right now is the final product.

It All Comes Down to This

Even though magic can be entertaining, it's also risky to learn. Why? Well when a magician does a trick, he or she knows how the trick works, but the audience doesn't. Once you know how the trick is done, you're on the opposite side and there's no turning back. So here's your final choice: Are you ready to step over to the other side? Are you willing to let other people have the same feeling you had when you first witnessed magic? Are you strong enough, deep down in your heart, to let go of that emotion? If you're not ready, don't worry about it. You can close this book right now, put it on your book shelf, and in a few years find it covered in dust. But if you're ready now, if you're strong enough, if you're willing to understand the illusions of life, well my fellow reader, welcome to my stage:

I Accept the Terms and Conditions.

About half of you probably skipped the introduction, as many readers do. If so, I suggest you flip back a few more pages and knock it out. If you don't want to read it, that's fine too, and I won't hold it against you. But then again, you are up against a man who has the potential to read your mind, steal your wallet, and turn you into a frog....in that order.

To be the person everyone looks at when you walk into the room, with all the publicity, and then be able to perform good quality magic is not an easy thing to do. Hopefully this section of the book can lessen the stress and nerves a beginner magician might have. When I first started to perform, my hands would shake in fear of messing up. But over the years it soon became second nature to me. I now carry a deck of cards with me everywhere I go. Some people question this odd behavior, but it's always good to be prepared just in case you randomly bump into your favorite celebrity!

Like I mentioned in the introduction, I'm not going to teach you how to be a world famous magician as it takes years of practice to understand every aspect of this art. Instead, I'm providing a book filled with tricks you can do anytime, anywhere, with minimum setup, and *look* like a professional magician to your audience. But first let's go through some basic "magic words" you'll commonly hear magicians use.

Basic Terminology

Audience View: The spectator's point of view or what the audience should be seeing.

Bottom Glimpse: Secretly looking and memorizing the bottom card.

Close-Up Magic: Performing magic for a small group of people, commonly using everyday objects.

Control: When the performer secretly moves a particular card to a specific location in the deck.

Cutting the Deck: Having an audience member pick up the top section of the deck and placing it next to the bottom section of the deck. Then taking the bottom section and placing it on top of the original top section.

Effect: The perceived outcome of a magic trick or what the audience believes is happening.

Exposed View: The performer's point of view.

Force: When the spectator believes they have a free choice, however the performer controls their choice.

Gimmick: An object that appears unaltered, yet has been altered to accomplish the magic trick.

Heckler: An audience member who tries to spoil the trick, or doesn't participate appropriately.

Illusion: In general, an object, event, or situation that can be perceived differently by others based on their own beliefs, despite what the reality may be.

Impromptu: Performing without setup.

Mentalism: A field of magic involving mind reading and predictions.

Misdirection: Distracting the audience while you secretly do something else.

Patter: A narrative that helps present the trick.

Perception: Our interpretation and awareness of a specific stimulus.

Prediction: A declaration revealing an outcome before it has occured.

Spectator: A specific person in the audience that the trick is for.

Shuffling: Mixing up the order of the cards in the deck.

Street Magic: Performing magic on the streets, typically in urban areas (similar to close up magic).

Top Glimpse: Secretly looking and memorizing the top card.

The Tricks YOU Will Learn

You should probably know the tricks you learn in this book aren't my best. Additionally, these aren't necessarily the tricks I perform in shows. I figured if I taught you the tricks I normally perform, the majority of you wouldn't have the experience to perform them and those of you who **do** have the experience would know all of my secrets! But these tricks are some of my favorites. Developing and learning these tricks helped me create and perform more advanced ones. Without mastering these tricks first, I would not be at the level I am today.

These tricks are geared towards people who are just getting into the art of magic or magicians who want to add simple, yet effective tricks to their routines. Regardless, all of these tricks are impromptu and powerful. I **have** performed them and they **do** receive amazing reactions (every trick is explained in the view of a right-handed performer. Those who are left-handed can reverse the explanations as necessary).

The "Rules" of the Game

When you first start to enter the world of magic, you need to take this into consideration: Am I willing to bring value and keep up the integrity of the magic community? If you answered with a "No," then I think you have the wrong book. However, if you answered with a "Yes," all you need to do is practice, keep a secret, never perform the same trick for the same audience more than once, and connect with your audience on an effective level.

Practice. The majority of these tricks are relatively easy to perform, but that does not mean you shouldn't practice! Some of you will look at a trick, do the actual trick with the directions for the first time, and then start performing to your friends a few minutes later. That is NOT what you should do. These tricks are meant for you to take your time and apply your own presentation and ideas to the concepts before performing to a live audience. No one is born being incredible at magic....except for me.

Keep a Secret. Knowing how to do something clever doesn't mean you have to tell other people how you do it. If you give away your secret, it will spoil the mystery and enjoyment of the experience. So I ask you, from performer to future performer, please do not reveal the tricks. If someone asks you how something is done, just say (in a really confused manner while looking at the props): "Honestly, I have no idea. It...just...sort of...happens, I guess." Or you can make up an answer that is so complicated it literally doesn't make sense....even to you. People, surprisingly, want to be puzzled. As humans we like the "what if" situations. I can't really stop you from revealing the tricks, so I guess I'll have to trust you.

Same Trick for Same Audience is a No-No. NEVER perform the same trick to the same audience more than once (I capitalized the word NEVER for a reason). If you perform the same trick twice, the audience will know the outcome and will be looking for things they didn't look for the first time. If this happens, you're increasing your chances of being caught...probably by a million.

Connect and Form a Bond. Your ability to connect and present yourself effectively is one of the key traits in order to be successful in life. Not just with performing magic, but with other aspects of your life as well. Presentation represents who you are and what you stand for. As a result, people will either form a positive or negative perception of you when they first meet or see you. Interact. Communicate. Make fun of yourself. Anything that will entertain your audience, yet still have them trust you at the same time. If your presentation skills lack, your marketing ability will lack as well. In other words, make sure your audience remembers you in a positive way.

It's a Hard Life...

Sometimes, to a performer, a trick may seem great, but it may seem obvious to the audience. On the other hand, sometimes to a performer a trick may seem terrible, but it may seem amazing to the audience. This is why you can't be discouraged when your audience catches you. Just take it as a lesson and alter whatever you need to do to make the trick better for next time. Being caught on occasion is just part of growing as a performer.

The method of any type of magic trick or illusion seems obvious to the person performing it. It even seems as though you don't understand why the audience can be fooled so easily. Yet, you must realize that our brains have been taught to see things in a certain way during specific situations. Performers then use and take advantage of this concept through entertainment.

How to Perform

Before you start performing, understand magic is made up of:

1. *Psychology* (understanding how your audience thinks)
2. *Presentation* (how the audience perceives you/the trick)
3. *Sleight of Hand* (the movements to accomplish the trick)
4. *Misdirection* (distracting the audience while you secretly do something else)
5. *Trust* (let's face it: it's one of the most important qualities in any type of relationship)

But most of all, remember that magic is about having *fun*. Make sure you AND the audience members are having fun or performing any type of routine is useless.

My Biggest Pet Peeve

Always always always ACT NATURAL in everything you do. For example, when you perform, you have to think to yourself: would I do this type of action with this type of object even when I'm not performing? If it's a hard move to do, practice. If you need more misdirection, practice. If something looks abnormal, practice. Why? It will make you better.

Magic is about taking ordinary objects and performing extraordinary things with them. If your body movements are unnatural, it immediately takes away from the "magical" moment and people aren't impressed at all. Filming yourself when you perform is a good way to test this out. Grab a buddy and go down to a local park. Ask him to be the cameraman, walk around, and perform some tricks (make sure people agree to be on camera first). Go back to your house, watch yourself on film, and take notes on how you can become better for the future. Rather than performing larger and faster, you need to perform more casual, and thus more natural. In other words, every trick you perform can't look like a trick to the audience- this point cannot be stressed enough.

Audience Control

It is also important to know how to control an audience. You will always have hecklers trying to ruin your routine, but take this as an opportunity to entertain more. Suggestions?

Audience Member: "Hey, all you did was XYZ!"
Your Response: "Wait a minute, that's how it's done? I've been trying to figure that out for years now!"
or:
Audience Member: "Hey! I saw what you did there!"
Your Response: "Oh, don't worry! I saw what I did as well!"

These responses will receive a good chuckle from the rest of the audience and hopefully the person who comments in the middle of your show will realize you know how to control a crowd. Yet, always remember that outsmarting people is not your goal. As soon as it feels like a challenge to win over your audience, stop performing.

Additionally, some people won't react to magic tricks and that's perfectly fine as well. There's no law stating every person needs to witness a magic trick sometime in their life (that would be pretty cool though). However, even if you know how to perform amazing tricks and would like to show everyone, you should learn when to stop. A few tricks are amazing. Lots of tricks are pushing it. If, at the end of your performance, people want to see more, you did a good job. Don't show every trick you know. You'll be in trouble and the audience will get bored after a while. Instead, pick a few good hard-hitting tricks and go. I probably know how to perform over one hundred tricks, but my show only consists of twenty. In my opinion, I would rather be an expert in twenty tricks than be average in one hundred.

Respect Everyone

Your Audience Members. Many magicians nowadays get caught up in their talent and don't realize that the spectator is the most important person in the room, not the performer. Therefore, performers need to treat their audience members like Kings and Queens. The more respect they receive, the more they will enjoy your presence.

Other Performers. Many people know at least one or two tricks they learned as a kid. This means that if you start to perform, most likely someone in the audience will ask if they can show you the trick(s) they know as well. If this occurs, step back, observe, and try to help them out afterwards. If the person is good, you can exchange some tricks and get better. But, no matter what, *always* be respectful to any performer. For instance, if you know (or think you know) how something is done, privately go up to the performer after the show and give your advice. In other words, don't be a heckler.

Another reason why you should respect your audience is because the nicer you are, the more people will end up liking you. The more people who like you, the more connections you will have. When it really comes down to it, the more connections you have in life, the higher and quicker up the ladder you will climb in any type of job you decide to pursue.

What's Your Reason?

Once you perform more, you can choose whether magic for you is a simple hobby, a form of social entertainment, a part-time job, or a profession. Overall, you should perform because you *want* to perform. Redundant, I know. Unfortunately, the end result for most performers has to be something tangible. Try to perform prepared to receive nothing in return, except for excited people wanting to see more.

Become the Conductor of Emotions

Your routines should create smiles, laughter, or even tears while you transform into the conductor of emotions. Remember that the moment the audience stops searching for explanations on how you accomplished the trick, they simply believe the magical moment.
Let's get started.

The Illusions & Tricks

One.
Imagination
-The Key Card-

"Too often we think about famous people who we feel have inspired us and too often we forget those who are closest to us that have inspired us the most. Who is most inspirational to me are my parents and what they taught me as I was growing up. From an early age, my parents taught me to always work hard and create high goals for myself. They taught me the importance of a strong work ethic. My parents taught me to never give up on my dreams and always to work toward achieving those dreams. Many times if I did not meet my goals on the first try I wanted to end my pursuit of that goal, but my parents would not let me, no matter how difficult it was for me to achieve. They wanted me to see the importance of working as hard as possible at attempting to meet my goals. It was important to me that I write about my inspirational figures who are close to me and I am lucky enough to have two inspirational figures that have helped shape me into who I am today. In closing, for that I will be forever grateful for what I have learned from my parents." -Steven Rodday

What have you always wanted to be since you were little? Travel back in time for a moment when you were five years old. Did you want to become a singer? Did you want to become an astronaut? Did you want to become a professional athlete? After all of these years, what are you now? Are you the same thing you wanted to be when you were five years old? If so, that's great and keep pursuing your childhood dream. If not, what has changed in your life that made you decide on something else? Regardless, would the five year old version of yourself be proud of where you are in your life right now?

Personally, I've always wanted to become a superhero. My Dad actually convinced me when I was a little boy that he was Superman-I'm not joking. He still believes he is to this day and I wouldn't recommend debating him over the subject because he will convince you otherwise. Although I realized the disappointing truth a few years later (don't tell him I said that!), this joke he pulled on me had a major impact on the way I would think in the future: the idea of super powers.

My Mom had a major impact on my magic career as well. When I was young, she bought me a magic kit and videos for my birthday and I was instantly hooked. I realized I could now be a magic superhero! As you can tell, I was a normal little boy...

While being a superhero, I would walk around my neighborhood "fighting crime." As I created scenarios in my head, my imagination would only flourish. However, I soon realized that running up and down the neighboorhood street in a superhero cape wasn't appropriate at the age of seventeen and my parents told me to stop and start applying to college.

All jokes aside, when I perform magic, some people believe I have real powers. For me, their reactions bring me back to the time when I thought I had actual powers. If the audience is inspired by my performance, I don't have to run around pretending I'm a superhero anymore. I have brought my audience back to their childhood where they believed anything was possible using their imagination. This reason alone makes me feel like a real hero.

One of the best things about being young is that we don't let the facts get in the way of our imagination. As we grow older, it becomes more difficult to think of a fictional story on the spot as we let predetermined notions get in the way of our creativity. As adults, we think too much about the next step, whereas children use their imagination to live for the moment. Many people nowadays fail to recognize that creativity is one of the key elements that helps us solve problems, take risks, and design new innovation.

Do you think it will ever be too late to pursue your childhood dream? I think it's about finding your imagination you once possessed as a child. And how can you bring this imagination back out of yourself? Well, one way is experiencing and performing the art of magic.

Name of Effect: "The Key Card"
Beginner Card Trick

Basic Effect: After a playing card is freely chosen, the performer can read the spectator's mind and reveal the selection.

What the Audience Sees: A card is freely chosen and placed back into the deck by the spectator. After the deck is thoroughly shuffled by one of the audience members, the performer turns his back and instantly reads the audience member's mind.

Background: Throughout my years of performing, I've always loved the idea of the audience handling the deck after someone selects a card. This gives an impression that the performer can't manipulate the card to a certain position in the deck and it also gives the spectator complete control of the deck. It addition, it limits the idea that sleight of hand is used to accomplish the trick and it really gives an extra boost to the overall routine. Think about it: let's say a performer had *you* choose a card, *you* placed it wherever *you* wanted, and *you* got to shuffle the deck. Wouldn't you feel that you're in complete control?

Method: Before you perform, memorize the bottom card. This is known as a "Key Card" because it will help you locate the selected card. You are now ready to perform the trick (Figure 1.1 Exposed View).

Spread the cards face down for your audience and have any audience member take one out. The card should be shown to the other audience members, but make sure you don't see it (Figure 1.2 Audience View).

After this is done, gather the cards back into one pile. Then, have the spectator place the selected card on top of the deck face down (Figure 1.3 Audience View).

Next, ask the audience member to cut the deck. If done correctly, the bottom card should now be on top of the selected card, but both cards somewhere in the middle. You can have the audience cut the deck as many times as they want after they do it the first time. However, the key card you memorized prior to performing and the card they selected will still be together. This is a way for the audience to believe they are shuffling the deck.

Once the audience is satisfied with their cuts, take the deck and spread the cards on the table, left to right face up, so everyone can see all the cards. As you do this, tell the audience member to make sure their card is somewhere in the deck and there is no way you know where or what the selection could be. While talking, you are looking for the key card you remembered in the beginning. If done correctly, THEIR selected card should be on the RIGHT SIDE of the card you memorized in the beginning. Once you've found it, you know their selection (Figure 1.4 Audience/Exposed View).

As soon as you realize what their card is, gather the deck back together and place it to the side. Since you know their card, you can now prove to your audience that you have supernatural powers. Ask the audience member to repeat the color of the card in their head. Wait a few seconds and say what color he or she is thinking. After that, you can narrow it down more. For instance, you could then ask to repeat the suit in their head, and then finally the value of their card. It will seem like you're reading their mind!

Let's sum it up:

1. Memorize the bottom card before you perform.

2. Have the selected card placed on top.

3. The audience cuts the deck as many times as they want, causing the selected card and the memorized card to be next to each other.

4. Spread the deck out, left to right face up, asking the audience if they see their card as YOU secretly locate the memorized card.

Figure 1.1 Exposed View

Figure 1.2 Audience View

5. The selected card should be on the right side of the card you memorized in the beginning.

6. Shave your head, buy a wheelchair, and pretend you're Professor X (a comic book character that can read minds).

Presentation Ideas/Alternative Methods/Tips:

"Hi Chris, can I show you a new card trick I've been working on? Great, thanks. Please take out any card you want for me. That one? Perfect.

"If you could show everyone the card and make sure you memorize it, that would be great. You can place it right on top of the deck afterwards.

"Now Chris, what I need you to do is cut the deck wherever you want so your card is lost somewhere in the middle. Great! Now I need you to cut the deck a few more times so no one knows the location of the card. I'll now take the deck and spread it on the table face up. Your selection is lost somewhere in the middle and there's no way I would know where or what your card is (look for your key card from the beginning. After you locate this, the selected card should be on the right side of it. Remember: this will only work if you spread the cards face up left to right).

"Chris, I'm going to turn my back. Since my back is turned, I can't see where you're looking. I need you to stare at your selected card and focus on the color of the card. Repeat it in your head. I'm sensing you're looking at a black card. Now I need you to think of the suit. Hmm...are you thinking of a spade? Okay, now I need you to think of the value of the card. Keep repeating it in your head. Are you thinking of the Ace of Spades?"

There are a few ways the audience could try and fool you. One way is if a person tries to select the bottom card in the beginning. Well, if he or she does that you're in great shape! You already know what

Figure 1.3 Audience View

Figure 1.4 Audience/Exposed View

that card is so you can really mess with their heads. Another way the audience will try and fool you is if he or she stares at the wrong card while your back is turned.

When I turn my back as I perform this trick, I tell them to stare at their card. A few seconds later I ask, "Wait a minute, are you looking at the correct card?" If the audience member is staring at the wrong card (trying to fool you), then he or she will be more impressed that you knew they were looking at the wrong card. If the audience member is looking at the correct card, just continue the trick as usual.

To make the trick more impressive, you could put your hands cupped over your eyes while you fan the deck onto the table. This way, you can't see your audience member's eyes, but you can still see the cards. Also, if it helps you more, you could memorize the bottom AND the top card. In this case, their selected card will be trapped between the bottom and the top card when you fan the cards face up.

Most likely this won't happen, but if the card you memorized in the beginning, the key card, is on the bottom of the deck when you fan the cards out (after the audience has cut the deck more than once), then the selected card is on top of the deck. Good luck.

Two.
Talent
-All About You-

"It is important to appreciate the views of others. We all develop our own truths and beliefs based on the things we've seen, heard, and experienced in our lives. It is important to be passionate about those truths and beliefs, but it is equally important to respect those perspectives of others. Their experiences have made them passionate about their truths and beliefs as your experiences have made you about yours. There is not necessarily a right and a wrong for everything and no one has all the answers. This is why it is important to communicate with opposing views, because it is through communication and open discussion that understanding and appreciation can occur." -Stephen Hegarty

So far we talked about the imagination we possessed at a young age. When we use our imagination effectively, most of us find our talents in life as well. For instance, we experiment with different clubs and activities to see where our strengths and weaknesses are. But sometimes we forget the actual talent we have can have a negative impact on our lives and alter society's definition of who we are as a person.

Think about it: no matter where you go, you always have people commenting on your talent(s) and soon it becomes stuck inside your head like a parasite. When you have people cheering your name when you walk into the room, the fame can get to your head. But when the lights go down and the cheering stops, you should be able to distinguish your friends from your fans.

Do you want people calling you "Magic Man" or something to that extent? Or would you rather have people actually know your real name? When you have a talent, more people start noticing you and some may only talk to you because you have that specific talent. When this occurs, you have to think to yourself: "If I lost this talent, would people still like who I am as a person?" This is why you can't let a talent define who you are. Having a talent is great and all, but what other great qualities do you possess?

When you start to become good at something, and attractive young folks are surrounding you, don't convince yourself that they enjoy who you actually are; they might be talking to you only because they want to see more of your talent. As a result, if you have a specific talent, be careful as it can bring you down this trap where you can't distinguish if the person you are talking to likes you for your talent or for your personality and other intangibles. Nevertheless, magicians are here to alter perspectives. Don't let your own magic tricks (or talents) alter your own perspective of who you truly are. Nobody likes an arrogant performer.

So what's one way to avoid the dark side? Don't tell the entire truth about your talents and accomplishments whenever they come up in conversation. If you're asked a question about what your talents are, describe your victories in dismissive terms as if they were a result of luck in addition to exaggerating your flaws. When you downplay your accomplishments, you make people feel better about theirs. However, altering perceptions about yourself in order to make productive illusions about others is a talent all its own.

Name of Effect: "All About You"
Beginner Card Trick

Basic Effect: The spectator stops dealing cards whenever he or she wants and the card he or she stops at is the matching card the performer predicted from the beginning.

What the Audience Sees: The performer tells the audience he will take out a "Prediction Card" and no one will know what it is, except for the performer. After he places the prediction card to the side, he has an audience member name any number between one and fifty-two, which the audience member then deals out one by one face down from the top of the deck onto the table. When the audience member takes the last card that was dealt out, it matches the prediction!

Background: This routine is based on a famous trick called "Any Card at Any Number." From what I have researched, there is no founder of this idea, but there are many variations. One is performed by Andrew Gerard called "Extraordinary Proof" which can be watched on the *True Astonishment Series* by Paul Harris. The basic idea is that the spectator, free of will, can pick any number between one and fifty-two and their selected card is in that position in the deck. In this case, I'm teaching you the prediction version instead.

Other methods people have created contain prep work or card forcing. However, with the prediction version, magicians can focus on their presentation, whether they perform it as a comedy routine or as a true mentalist.

Method: First, tell the spectator that this trick is all about them. While doing this, ask the spectator to shuffle the deck as well. Afterwards, take the deck back and say you will make a prediction. All you need to do is look at the top card and find its matching card. Next, place the matching card next to you face down and tell the audience this will be the "Prediction Card" (Figure 2.1 Exposed View).

Wait, what is a "matching card"? Good question. Well a deck of cards is made up of black and red faces. Then, there are two suits for each color. We have the red half of the deck, made from the hearts and diamonds, and the black half of the deck, made from the clubs and spades. Let's say the top card is the ace of hearts. In this case, you would remove the ace of diamonds and set it to the side face down. All you're doing here is taking whatever numerical value the top card is and taking out the same numerical value of the same color (hearts: diamonds; clubs: spades).

Figure 2.1 Exposed View

Figure 2.2 Audience/Exposed View

Figure 2.3 Audience View

Ask your audience to select a number between one and fifty-two and YOU (the performer) deal that number of cards from the top of the deck (*one by one face down*) onto the table. For explanation purposes, let's say the spectator chooses the number ten. As you deal out ten cards, the first card you put on the table is actually the original top card of the deck. This card now becomes the *last* (or bottom card) in the pile of ten you are creating (Figure 2.2 Audience/Exposed View).

When you finally reach the tenth card in the deck, flip it over so it is face up. Obviously the tenth card will NOT be the matching card of your prediction, but keep in mind the audience doesn't know this. Pause for five seconds, peek at your prediction card (still not letting anyone see it) and sit there confused. After five seconds of acting, shake your head and say "Oh yes, this trick is dedicated to you, I forgot. Here, I need YOU to deal the cards out." At this point, gather the ten cards that were dealt out, place them back onto the deck, hand the deck to the spectator, and ask him or her to deal out ten cards (one by one face down) from the top like you previously did (Figure 2.3 Audience View). As a result, the tenth card in the deck is *now* the matching card to the prediction (the original top card) (Figure 2.4 Exposed View).

Hand the deck to the spectator and have him or her deal out ten cards this time (or whatever number they choose). If done correctly, the original top card should now be on top of the pile. The audience won't realize you just re-ordered the cards because your "mistake" will draw attention away from it. However, please do this naturally and casually. Finally, with a dramatic ending, have the spectator turn over the "last card they dealt out" (the top card of the pile) and show them that the tenth card matches your prediction! (Figure 2.5 Audience View).

Let's sum it up:

1. Tell the audience before you perform that this trick is all about them.

2. After an audience member shuffles the cards, fan out the deck (to yourself) and tell them you will take out a prediction.

Figure 2.4 Exposed View

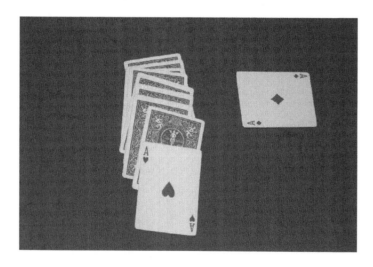

Figure 2.5 Audience View

3. Find the "matching card" to the top card and put that to the side face down.

4. Ask the spectator to name a number between one and fifty-two.

5. Deal that many cards onto the table face down and flip over the last card you deal out.

6. Act confused and pretend you messed up, but the audience doesn't know why.

7. Come to a realization that you said beforehand the trick is all about them so THEY should deal the cards out

8. Gather the ten cards (or whatever number was chosen) and place them back on top of the deck.

9. Hand the deck to the spectator and have him or her deal out ten cards (or whatever number was chosen) and flip over the "tenth" card.

10. Flip over your prediction and it should match!

Presentation Ideas/Alternative Methods/Tips:

"Good evening Joe. Before we continue, I want you to know this trick is all about YOU. Therefore, can YOU shuffle the deck of cards for me? Just let me know when you're done.

"Great. I'm going to look through the cards and take out a prediction (fan the cards to yourself and look at the top card. Next, take out the matching card to the top card).

"Now Mr. Joe, I need YOU to name ANY number between one and fifty-two. You like the number ten? Okay, I'll deal out ten cards from the top of the deck face down (after dealing them out, flip over the tenth card).

"Umm...wait a minute....I don't think I did this trick correctly (peek at prediction). Yeah, um...I think I messed up. Oh wait! This trick is about YOU! I forgot! How about YOU deal ten cards out? (Gather the ten cards and place them back on top of the deck. Hand the deck to the spectator to deal out).

"Flip over the tenth card for me please. As you can see, when YOU did it, the tenth card was....a red Ace. My prediction: The other red Ace."

When you perform this trick, I highly suggest using a gap of numbers. For instance, you could say "Please select a number between 10 and 30. Anything below 10 seems too low and anything above 30... well... we'll be here all day." Using lines like this puts a little comedy into the routine.

Advanced Version:

For people out there who perform magic for a living: obtain a pinky break on the last card of the pile (the first card they dealt out) and pass it to the top with misdirection. If you're a professional magician, I HIGHLY suggest you try it that way. You can easily do this with an "Any Card at Any Number" routine and have the audience member deal the cards in your hand. It's a beautiful illusion and one of my favorite tricks to perform. Good luck.

Three.
Love
-The Object Prediction-

"Live your life slowly. It's cliche, but smell the roses, enjoy the little moments, and appreciate the people. Spread love to them, and make solid relationships. Learn to forgive, and write thank you cards. Go outside your comfort zone to do a nice gesture, it can only do good. Remember that every kind of people is a person. Build up those people and fill your life with love. In the end, if you have loved, you have lived." -Amanda Tiedtke

Once we determine what our talents are in life, most of us are old enough to experience "love." It is within these years that our perception of "love" can change day to day. Society has tried to tell us what love should feel like, yet we never know what to believe for ourselves. As a result, one of the greatest (and complicated) illusions people create for themselves (*especially* at a young age), yet cannot always control, is their idea of love.

What is "love"? Is it the missing piece in your life that you didn't even know was missing? Or is it the end of an individual journey to create a new collective one? How do you know you "love" someone?

The illusion of love is that it's too easy to think you're actually in love. For instance, things that look like love (talking about a specific person obsessively, daydreaming, or listening to mushy music) is when Love comes into our lives, only as a sly actress, while making us think we have passionate feelings for someone. At times, once a person falls into the arms of Love, their destiny is at stake because all of their divergent emotions suddenly converge on a single presence. Is this considered a good or bad thing? Or both?

The majority of us become anxious trying to correctly predict the outcome of our own future as we continuously search for "the one." When this occurs, we either find someone and stay with that person forever or break up with that person in the future and continue our search. Does this mean we only "date" others to find our strengths and weaknesses for when we finally find "the one"? Is this considered a good or bad thing? Or both?

Well, how do we solve this illusion? How do we find "the one"? Here's one possibility: stop looking for the love of your life. They will be there waiting for you when you're doing the things you love. When you're pursuing your passions in life, you're not trying to act like someone else to impress another person and there should be nothing to stress out about. Other parts of your life will fall into place in your favor if you love what you're doing and living the life *you* want to live.

The power of love and the power of magic are two of the most dangerous, non-tangible weapons anyone could have in life. Once you experience one of them, you never look at life the same. And, if you experience both, well, you are one lucky person.

Name of Effect: "The Object Prediction"
Beginner Mind Trick

Basic Effect: The performer predicts exactly what the spectator is thinking of.

What the Audience Sees: The performer brings out a box of playing cards, a book, and a cell phone. The performer asks the spectator to think of any item. After the spectator reveals his or her thought, the performer tells the audience he predicted something before he arrived to perform. The performer reveals his prediction and it is exactly right.

Background: This is mind-reading at its best. The spectator is thinking of any item and the performer predicts what the object was going to be beforehand. How can it get any better than that?

Method: You have three predictions located in three different spots. Pretty clever, huh? You can use any objects you want, as many objects as you want, and as many predictions as you want. For explanation purposes, we can stick to a box of playing cards, a book, and a cell phone (Figure 3.1 Audience View).

Before you perform the trick, take a random playing card and write on the back "You will choose the card box." Place this card into an empty card box (Figure 3.2 Exposed View).

Next, take a notecard and write "You will choose the book." Place this notecard on the inside cover of the book (Figure 3.3 Exposed View).

Finally, take a blank piece of paper and write "You will choose the phone." Take a picture of the piece of paper with your phone and save the picture. Before you perform, make sure the screen has this picture on it, but place the phone on the table so the screen is face down (Figure 3.4 Exposed View)

Let's sum it up:

1. Prepare everything above.

2. Place all of these items on the table and have an audience member think of any one of the three displayed items.

3. Whatever item the spectator chooses, reveal that prediction and ignore the other predictions.

Presentation Ideas/Alternate Methods/Tips:

"Hi Mary, can I show you something interesting? I have three items here: a box of playing cards, a book, and a cell phone. What I need you to do is think of any item displayed here.

Figure 3.1 Audience View

Figure 3.2 Exposed View

"I'll give you five seconds to make up your mind. I want to make sure this is a free choice.

"5...4...3...2...1...ready?

"For the first time, can you reveal what object you were thinking of? The book? Would you like to change your mind? No? Well it's really interesting you chose the book because before I got here, I made a prediction. I don't want to touch anything, so I need you to please open up the book to the first page and reveal what it says."

Many performers would ask an audience member "Are you sure?" rather than "Would you like to change your mind?" when an audience member has the freedom to select an object. Asking the audience member if they are "sure" about something may be confusing because of course they are sure! Since they were the one who made the decision, why are you asking them if they are sure about their decision? By asking the audience member if they would like to "change their mind" lessens the stress during the decision making process and it makes the audience member a star rather than a victim.

Obviously you can perform this trick with as many objects as possible, but that means you need to think of creative ways to reveal the predictions. In addition, NEVER perform this trick more than once to the same group of people. They will INSTANTLY figure it out.

This is a perfect trick to open up with, but I'm going to warn you now that a lot of people might ask you what the lottery numbers are going to be afterwards. Good luck.

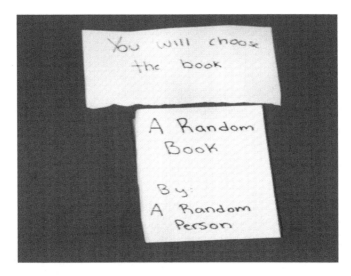

Figure 3.3 Exposed View

Figure 3.4 Exposed View

Four.
Passion
-The Marvel-

"Find your passion in life and make a career out of it. Do not settle for anything or anybody. If you do happen to make a career out of a passion you have, know that you are in the minority. If you are fortunate enough to make this dream come true, never forget that you have been given one of the most special gifts life could ever offer." -Michael Patch

The previous chapters talked about imagination, talent, and love. Specifically, according to the last chapter, in order to find "the one" (the love of your life), you need to pursue your own personal passions. But how do you find these passions to begin with? Maybe these questions will help:

1. Can this activity allow you to enhance your creativity using your *imagination*?
2. Do you have a *talent* (or do you want to have a talent) for this activity?
3. Do you *love* this activity so much that you could pursue it for the rest of your life without being paid?

If you have an activity that you do, and you answered "Yes" to all three questions, then I believe you have a passion as well.

Another question to consider is this: when you're performing a task someone else told you to perform, do you often daydream about doing another activity? If so, what is the other activity you'd rather be doing? The activity you're imagining yourself doing instead could also be your passion.

After you find your passion, try and pursue it as much as possible. Why? Well, when people are passionate about something, they use their passions to create work that is unique and different. Most of the time, they're so good that it's hard for people to ignore them.

Understand that you create yourself based on your personal passions. The culture today will try to take these things and modify them. Working on something is hard, but when you have passion for it, it makes it a lot easier and you become more creative. Stop chasing opportunities that aren't unique to you, but chase the ones that cry out for your passions. You can either conform to the culture or defy it. It's up to you.

Name of Effect: "The Marvel"
Intermediate Mind Trick

Basic Effect: The performer can read the mind of an audience member and reveal what card they are thinking of without touching the deck.

What the Audience Sees: The performer turns away from the audience while the audience member chooses one card and shows everyone else. The performer then divines the selection.

Background: This trick is also in the book titled *The Everything Card Tricks Book* by Dennis Rourke. Many performers don't take advantage of using *other* people to help them accomplish a trick. It's a great method and the possibilities are endless. In other words, this trick involves a secret partner.

Method: This works best with a large crowd, especially on stage. Once the audience member thinks of a card, you want him or her to write it down so everyone else can see. Or if you want to do it in a small setting, tell an audience member to take the deck, shuffle it up as much as they want, scatter the cards across the table face down, and take one out....all while your back is turned. Once you turn back around, your partner in the audience will give you signals on what the selected card is. The table on the next page is what your partner should do once he or she knows the card. It won't matter if he or she is sitting or standing because the signals should still work. For this type of communication, the right hand tells the value of the card whereas the left hand tells the suit of the card.

Let's sum it up:

1. With your back turned around, have an audience member freely select a card without any possibility of you knowing what it is and have them show the selection to the audience (make sure your partner sees it).

2. As you turn back around, casually look at your partner, and they will give you a signal on what the selected card is. Afterwards, reveal the card in a unique/creative way.

Presentation Ideas/Alternate Methods/Tips:

There are three things you should take into consideration when choosing a partner: 1. They have to be sneaky 2. They have to be trustworthy and 3. They have to know the signals like it's second nature to them (you don't want them to accidentally give you the wrong signal). If you're not a fan of these signals, you can also use the signals from "252" (another trick in this book) to guess the value of the card. However, if you go this route, you and your partner need to think of other signals to represent a ten, jack, queen, king, and the suits.

In addition, have your friend give you the signal as soon as you walk back in the room. Once he or she gives you the signal, you should somehow give your partner a signal letting him or her know that you received their signal. This way, your friend won't be in the same position throughout the entire trick.

Also, your friend should ACT like an audience member. Do not have him or her be on stage with you or standing next to you while you do this trick. The other audience members should have no idea that your friend is helping you out, as they should believe you are the only performer. In other words, do not draw ANY attention to your partner, because the more natural the routine looks, the better reactions you will receive.

Finally, make sure your partner REACTS like everyone else. Your partner doesn't need to yell at the top of their lungs or be the quiet mouse, but just have him or her blend in with the crowd. Afterwards, make sure you THANK your partner. You don't want him or her to get jealous and give away the secret!

If you use this as a close up trick rather than a stage trick, have the audience member place the card face down on the table. Next, go up to the card, start smelling it, and then reveal it after a few "sniffs". When people ask you how you can "smell" cards, you can respond with "As for the number, I usually guess. But if the card is red, it smells like strawberries or cherries. If the card is black, it smells like blackberries or burnt pizza." Good luck.

The Signals:

Card Value	Right Hand Position
Ace	Thumb against chin
2	Thumb and forefinger on chin
3	Thumb and two fingers on chin
4	Thumb and three fingers on chin
5	Thumb and four fingers on chin
6	Hand at side or in lap with thumb extended
7	Hand at side or in lap with thumb and forefinger extended
8	Hand at side or in lap with thumb and two forefingers extended
9	Hand at side or in lap with thumb and three fingers extended
10	Hand at side or in lap with thumb and four fingers extended
Jack	Hand at belt
Queen	Hand scratching shoulder
King	Hand scratching head

Card Suit	Left Hand Position
Clubs	Closed fist
Hearts	Over heart
Spades	Flat and straight
Diamonds	Knuckles up, as if showing a ring

Five.
Dreams
-Black Hole-

"Peace." -Ronald Glennon

You need to wake up now. This isn't real. You're going to be late in the morning.

What was your reaction when you read those sentences? Next time you're bored go up to someone and say that and let me know how they react. I'm sure many people would believe you for a split second. Why? Because a dream (or even the concept of waking up) could easily be considered one of life's greatest surprises.

After we have determined what our passion are, we tend to want more control over things we can't have control over, such as our dreams at night. However, are dreams just a nonsense byproduct of our sleeping brain, or a window into our unconscious mind enriched with revelations? Although dreams can create their own scenarios, it gives people the slightest hope that these scenarios may or may not come true. Other than yourself, no one has the ability to enter this secret world, unless you let them.

If you had the power to dream anything at night, what would you dream of? Imagine you had the ability to condense any amount of time into a few hours of sleep. Would you design a new innovative life? The majority of you would dream of more adventurous things, like being a superhero, rescuing princesses, and sword fighting soldiers. Yet, if you had this ability, how extreme would you take this?

You know, deep down, you will eventually wake up, right? When you finally awake, you will look in the mirror and wonder if this person is actually you or some type of figure waiting for the next exciting conflict so you can be the protagonist. Most likely you will go back to sleep and experience every opportunity your mind can think of.

Having complete control would be enjoyable at first, don't get me wrong. But after a while, your creativity will start to lack and your dreams will become mundane and less exciting. Would you actually want the ability to consciously control your dreams each night? Or do you enjoy that feeling when you close your eyes before falling asleep and knowing the adventure you'll soon be experiencing will be a complete surprise?

When we wake up from these dreams, there is a moment, just before everything happens, when simply to be awake again, and still alive, is unexpected. Is it because prior to that very moment, you were sleeping and therefore not alert enough to be able to predict you were about to wake up? When you go to sleep, why do you always feel a guarantee you will wake up again? Even though waking up might be the main event of our everyday lives, we never actually see it coming. I guess that is the paradox of sleep: you don't know you fell asleep until you wake up.

As we "die off for the day" our humanity rises since there's nothing, while sleeping, we can do to stand out- no action we can take to set ourselves apart from others. But here's the thing: how do you know, right now, at this specific moment, that you're awake? How do you know you're not dreaming of being awake? Is it possible to prove that everything surrounding you right now aren't just figments of your own imagination?

We must always embrace and value the unexpected events in our lives. One way our brain makes decisions is creating an educated guess as to what comes next based off assumptions and past experiences. Surprises prevent us from predicting events and the problem with predictability is that we anticipate the ending. Many people would love to know their future, but the concept of the unknown is one of the greatest motivators in life.

Name of Effect: "Black Hole"
Intermediate Coin Trick

Basic Effect: A spectator's signed coin visually penetrates through a card case.

What the Audience Sees: A spectator signs a coin. Afterwards, a drinking glass and a card case come into play. The card case is placed on the mouth of the cup. The performer then takes the signed coin and places it in his palm. He slams the coin on top of the card case and the coin visually travels through the card case and the spectator can see it drop to the bottom of the glass.

Background: Although there are various methods out there, I believe this is the most simple and direct one. There is no set up, special gimmicks, or duplicate coins and with enough practice, any level of magician can perform this trick as well.

Method: For this illusion, you need a coin, a closed card case with cards inside, and a glass. You can also use a wallet or some other type of rectangular object that can go over the mouth of a glass instead of a card case. In order to receive the best reactions, I would recommend using a small clear glass. The height of the glass should also be close to the height of the card case. I'll wait until you fetch those objects and then you can follow along.

Got them? Sweet. Now place the glass on the table (Figure 5.1 Audience View). Next, take the card case and place it on top of the mouth so its covering the majority of the mouth of the glass. However, don't have the deck completely centered. If done correctly, there should be a small opening in the back between the card case and the mouth of the glass.

You need to push the card case up towards the front (just a little) so the opening is only seen through the back. When you push it forward, it will also cause the gap in the back to increase (Figure 5.2 Exposed View)

If you placed the case on top of the glass correctly, the opening will not be seen by the front view. When you perform, you have to make

Figure 5.1 Audience View

Figure 5.2 Exposed View

Figure 5.3 Audience View

Figure 5.4 Exposed View

sure that the spectators aren't standing up with a bird's eye view (or directly standing/sitting on your left or right hand side) or else they will easily see the opening between the card case and the back of the glass (Figure 5.3 Audience View).

The penetration aspect is the trickiest part of the illusion. You need to place the coin on your palm, but on the lower part near your wrist (the coin should be about a half an inch near your wrist). Do not have the coin centered in your palm because the coin won't fit in the gap you created in the back.

After you established the placement of the coin on your hand, take your opposite hand and place your pointer finger on the center of the case. This creates stability on the case so when you slam the coin between the gap, the case or the glass will not move. The spectator will not think anything of this, trust me (Figure 5.4 Exposed View).

Next, slam your hand down on the card box letting the coin fall into the gap. If you practice in the mirror with a table, it looks like you slammed the coin right through the card case.

Although the method is pretty simple, you must have the correct angle and presentation in order to perform this well. You need the audience to believe you actually slammed the coin through the card case. Especially if everything is borrowed, it brings a stronger impact to the overall illusion.

Let's sum it up:

1. Borrow a coin, a card box, and a small glass.

2. As the audience member signs the coin, place the card box on the glass, but leave a small gap in the back.

3. Place the signed coin in your hand near your wrist.

4. Using your free hand, keep your finger on the card box for support.

5. Slam the card box and the coin should fall through the gap.

Presentation Ideas/Alternate Methods/Tips:

"Hi there, can I please borrow your wallet? Thank you. I'll try not to make your credit card disappear. No promises though.

"In addition to your wallet, is there a possibility you have a coin on you? A nickel or quarter will work best.

"I have a marker here. What I need you to do is sign the coin.

"I want you to make sure that I'm not switching the coin in any way. I can see that you finished your drink and your glass is empty. Do you mind if I borrow it for a moment?

"I'll take your wallet and place it on top of your empty glass just like this. The coin will be placed into my hand as well. Now watch this. SLAM.

"Here is your coin and wallet, sir. I would hold onto those if I were you. They seem pretty magical to me."

What I do immediately after the penetration is remove the wallet or card case. I don't want any evidence showing there was a gap between the wallet or the card case and the glass. Someone might get too excited and look on the other side quickly.

Another great way to perform this is to not physically slam the coin through, but secretly slide it through the back gap using your thumb. First, make sure there's a small gap in the back of the glass (it doesn't need to be as big compared to the slam version). Next, place the coin on the card case in the center. Cover the coin with your hand, but have your hand vertical. From the audience point of view, your four fingers should be in front of the coin. Using your thumb, slide the coin backwards into the gap. While you're doing this, pretend you are rubbing the coin. Once the coin drops into the glass, rub the card case for a split second and lift up your hand. In this version it seems that you rubbed the coin through the card case (the only finger that should be moving is your thumb if you choose to use this method). Oh yeah, and make sure you don't slam the coin too hard or you'll break the glass! Good luck.

Six.
Intelligence
-Two-Fifty-Two-

"Most people are afraid of failure. It chokes them, locks them in their routine. Most people don't see the beauty in it. In failing. In taking a risk. But life is built on failure. It is at the core of individuality. We are not perfect. We never will be. It's a beautiful thing." -Brendan Stone

As we finally wake up in the morning from leaving our own world, we come to recognize that our dreams tend to enhance our creativity and motivation. How? Well, we never knew those scenarios could ever occur in the first place. As a result, we try new things that we've never done before. However, before we go exploring, we must have the correct "education."

Now of course we want to excel in education because it gives us an opportunity to learn and explore *more*. Yet, many people fail to recognize that you can define education in many ways. For example, why did you read this specific book in the first place? What's the point of reading my ideas and tricks? Should you even be reading this book? Are my thoughts worth learning?

Education is one of the determinants of who we are, what we will do with our future, and how we will react to situations. The creativity we have to find within ourselves is equally important as the literacy we learn in institutions. These types of facilities teach us to be successful in life and, to an extent, never be (for a lack of a better word) "wrong."

We have been trained to make the correct choices for the better part of ourselves and our surroundings throughout our life. As most of us grow older, we tend to lose this gift of creativity that was lacking in our education and have a mental breakdown when we become "wrong." But sometimes we're not necessarily "wrong" when we can't find the "correct" answer. All we need to do is look at the situation from a different perspective which could ultimately improve the knowledge and creativity we have already established within ourselves. In other words, some of the innovations we use today actually started from "mistakes" people *thought* they made.

Name of Effect: "252"
Intermediate Mind Trick

Basic Effect: The performer knows the number an audience member is thinking of.

What the Audience Sees: The performer asks a group of people to think of a number between one and nine. As they do, the performer leaves the room. When the performer returns, he immediately reveals what number the group has chosen.

Background: There are so many ways you could accomplish this "mind reading" trick. The idea I'm about to explain is actually based off an old trick my grandfather taught me when I was little (needless to say, we fooled A LOT of people with it). His original method used a piece of paper and a pencil, but I changed it up a bit to suit my performance. I wanted to think of an easy, yet fun way to fool people that contained absolutely nothing- except for a friend in the audience. This trick is dedicated to you Grandpa John.

Method: This works best with a large group of people, but you can perform it for as many as you want. As you read above, this trick does involve an "assistant" or "confederate."

The pictures provided show the signals, but I'll explain them as well. What your assistant needs is something they can hold in their hand. This should be an ordinary object such as a water bottle, pencil, or even a cell phone. Once the group has chosen the number, come back into the room and look at your friend for a split second while he or she is in the correct position corresponding to the selected number.

Let's sum it up:

1. If the group chooses the number one, your friend will hold the object in their right hand with the "top" of the object facing up (you and your friend can determine what the "top" of the object will be) (Figure 6.1 Exposed View).

2. If the group chooses the number two, your friend will hold the object with both hands near their waist, yet still having the "top" face upwards (Figure 6.2 Exposed View).

3. If the group chooses the number three, your friend will do the same thing as "1", however they will place the object in their left hand (Figure 6.3 Exposed View).

4. If the group chooses the number four, your friend will hold the object in their right hand, but this time the "top" will be facing outwards, pointing at you (Figure 6.4 Exposed View).

5. If the group chooses the number five, your friend will hold the object with both hands near their waist, but the "top" will be facing outwards, pointing at you (Figure 6.5 Exposed View).

6. If the group chooses the number six, your friend will hold the object with their left hand and the "top" will be facing outwards, pointing at you (Figure 6.6 Exposed View).

7. If the group chooses the number seven, your friend will hold the object in their right hand and the "top" will be facing downwards (Figure 6.7 Exposed View).

8. If the group chooses the number eight, your friend will hold the object with both hands near their waist and the "top" will be facing downwards (Figure 6.8 Exposed View).

9. If the group chooses the number nine, your friend will hold the "top" with their left hand and the object will be facing downwards (Figure 6.9 Exposed View).

Presentation Ideas/Alternate Methods/Tips:

You could also have your audience think of a two or three digit number. For example, as soon as you receive the signal/number from your partner, you could give your partner your signal letting him or her know you received the first number signal, and they could signal you for another number. Performing this way really freaks people out because there's no way you would be able to "read their mind" if the audience is thinking of a two or three digit number! Good luck.

252

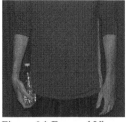
Figure 6.1 Exposed View

Figure 6.2 Exposed View

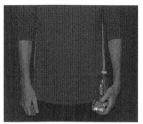
Figure 6.3 Exposed View

Figure 6.4 Exposed View

Figure 6.5 Exposed View

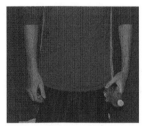
Figure 6.6 Exposed View

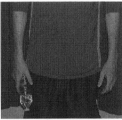
Figure 6.7 Exposed View

Figure 6.8 Exposed View

Figure 6.9 Exposed View

Seven.
Perfection
-Simplicity-

"Whenever possible, bring joy to the room." -John Hopkins

After society has formed its own perception of our "intelligence", it usually uses the same scale to judge us on how "perfect" we are, which can then impact our happiness. But we cannot always accept this.

Let's break it down for a second: what is the criteria you must have in order to be *happy*? How do you know if you're happy? What is your true definition of "happiness"?

We become unhappy when we dwell on the negative things and our expectations are too high and misplaced. I get it though since being happy can be hard at times. Why? Because we long to feel happier than those around us. Do you think we will ever possess true happiness if we are consistently jealous of what others have? Does this mean happiness is simply letting go of this jealousy?

Our culture creates our own obsession with happiness while at the same time taking away the true meaning behind it. If we were happy all the time, it would be impossible to cope with ourselves. Of course those times of happiness we possess--feeling confident and strong-- are wonderful. We should embrace and cherish these moments, since they do not come very often. But to think, just for a moment, those times will last forever is a dangerous thing, especially to the mind, since we mostly learn things by engaging with the hard, confusing, and sad moments in our lives.

There would be no such thing as happiness if there were no despondency. Be grateful for the bad events in your life for the happiness you could possess as a result in the near or far future. Just think of it this way: if losing something never hurt, then gaining something wouldn't feel so good.

Our struggle to be happy and perfect at every stage of life is a common element of the human condition. Society is always striving to build this "Utopian" world. The only way this would work is if we let go of all conventions of life--the laws, religions, and customs--and re-train our imagination to build new ones, perhaps based on different values. In this "perfect world", could we go one day trying to live without a clock? Could we go for one week trying to live without technology? Could we go for one month trying to live without the mirror?

As human beings, we cannot live without material, scientific, artistic, and moral needs. Yet, at the same time, we cannot meet all of these necessities through our own efforts. We sometimes look for answers in the customs and religions of the past. If we can't do that, we seek the help of others. For instance, when we lack self-fulfillment, we often rely on culture (from the past or the present) to help us achieve what we need to achieve. In a sense, most of us believe that society binds us to a "contract" as soon as we enter the world. Do you think it is ever possible to break free of this contract? Are we limited to what is considered "perfection"?

Accepting imperfection is part of accepting our humanity. I'm not trying to say don't be happy or pursue perfection because that would be ridiculous. Just realize when everything is perfect in life, there is nothing to strive for. Desiring what may seem to be "perfect", even when you don't quite know what it is and cannot do anything about it, is a common trait many humans possess.

Everyone seems to be searching for happiness and perfection. Yet, what are they? What exactly are we looking for?

Name of Effect: "Simplicity"
Beginner Card Trick

Basic Effect: The performer can find the spectator's card in the middle of the deck without any sleight of hand or peeks.

What the Audience sees: A freely selected card is taken out from the deck, looked at, and then placed back in. Immediately, without any sleight of hand, the performer looks through the deck and takes out the selection.

Background: This trick fools so many people, including professional magicians. Although it's easy and direct, people try so hard to figure out tricks and this technique rarely crosses their mind. It's the ultimate "pick a card...is this your card?" method. I absolutely love it.

One of my buddies showed me this card trick a while ago, but performed it differently. I loved the idea and turned it into something I've been using for awhile now. Although there is a little setup, it takes me about ten seconds (and sometimes I do it right in front of the audience while talking).

Method: Before you perform, separate the deck so all of the red cards are on one side of the deck and all of the black cards are on the other. Once you've done that, your setup is complete (Figure 7.1 Exposed View).

Next, ask a person to pick out any card they want. When you have them take out the card, remember if their card was from the upper half of the deck or the lower half of the deck. To make it easier on myself, I usually spread only the upper half to the audience and tell them to take any card (most likely, they will pick from the half you are spreading to them) (Figure 7.2 Audience View)

After they choose the card, ask them to remember it. While the audience member is looking at the card, spread the deck in your hand to whatever half their card did NOT come from. For example, if they chose a card from the upper half, spread the deck until you get to the lower half. Have the spectator place their card anywhere they want in that half. Once again, they will most likely put their card in the half

Figure 7.1 Exposed View

Figure 7.2 Audience View

you're spreading towards them (Figure 7.3 Audience View).

Remember: all of this happens with the cards face down in your hand and you're holding the entire deck, not just one half. Additionally, you shouldn't tell your audience that you want them to place their card in the opposite half. This process should look natural like you're just spreading the deck to them.

If the above happens correctly, all you need to do is look through the deck (make sure you're the only one looking because they will see the different colored cards organized) and fan until you see one card that is different from the rest of the cards. For instance, a red card will be mixed in with the black cards or vice versa. You can then work a presentation to "reveal" their card (Figure 7.4 Exposed View).

Let's sum it up:

1. Before you perform, separate the cards into red and black.

2. Have an audience member take out a card and memorize it (YOU remember if it came from the upper half or lower half).

3. Have the audience member place the card back in the opposite half they took it from (do this casually).

4. Look through the deck (make sure no one sees the cards except for you) and their card should stand out in front of all the other ones.

5. Read their minds and take out their card!

Presentation Ideas/Alternate Methods/Tips:

"Hey Jimmy take out any card you want out for me. That one? Perfecto.

"Please show everyone as I turn my back. Place it right here for me. All I'm going to do is look through the deck and I want you to repeat the card in your head. Hmm... okay....okay... I'm sensing your card was the five of hearts."

Figure 7.3 Audience View

Figure 7.4 Exposed View

There are a few different ways you can present this. This can either be a used as a simple trick to go to or it could be used to locate someone's card and then proceed to another reveal from there.

One tip I suggest is to make sure you know if the audience member picked a card from the top or bottom half of the deck. You can do this a few ways but I'll explain one I like:

Before I start the trick, I take a pencil and place a very light dot in the corner on the back of the card that separates the black and red cards. In this case, I know exactly where the black and red cards separate and the audience will never see the dot (I usually put the dots on one of the jokers. And hey, if they pick the card with the dot on it, you can immediately tell them they chose the joker!)

Once you separate the deck into red and black you can have one person shuffle one pile and another person shuffle the other pile face down. Then, bring both halves together and perform the trick. In this case, the audience believes the deck is actually shuffled; however the audience members were just mixing up the colored piles. After performing this trick, you could perform the trick titled "Colors" in this book as well.

When I perform, most people are looking for me to perform sleight of hand or look at another card to use as a key card, but you perform this entire routine with the deck face down, which is great (except when you look for their card obviously). You could even cut the deck a few times, but make sure you don't shuffle or it will mess up the color order.

Unless you plan on performing it more than once (which I don't recommend), right after you reveal their card, immediately shuffle up the deck to ruin the evidence that the cards were in order. You don't want someone to take the deck and look through it! Good luck.

Eight.
Criticism
-TnR-

"I love playing soccer. Some people may call me a soccaholic. However, when I think about it, the game of soccer is very similar to my life philosophy. Soccer is the ultimate team sport. No one can win the game all by themselves. I need to depend on my other teammates to help me accomplish my goals (pun intended), just like I need to depend on my friends and family to help me through difficult times. Sometimes we need to pass the ball backwards, in order to move it forwards. In life, sometimes we hit obstacles and challenges, but eventually we get through them with the help from those around us. There are so many decisions to be made during a soccer game: should I pass the ball or take a shot? In life, there are also many important decisions to be made. It definitely helps to be surrounded by people who are supportive. My life is greatly enriched by the people around me: my friends, my family and yes, even my soccer teammates. My name is Christine Fay and I'm proud to be a soccaholic."-Christine Fay

Some are afraid of it, others avoid it, and society has taught us to categorize it as a negative word. What am I talking about? Well, you've already learned how to pursue your passions and figure out what makes you happy, so now you're attempting to create some type of innovation. But here comes the hard part: *criticism.* The critics find the gaps in our first draft that we most likely wouldn't see ourselves. Understanding and accepting criticism is one of the most valuable tools in life if you want to be successful.

Even though it might be harsh, every suggestion, tip, or recommendation can be used to improve your future. You will meet at least one group of people in your lifetime that will tell you that you can't do something and you're wasting time. But when the same people stop talking to you, and deep down you know that you're doing something unproductive, it means you're in trouble. Why? Well, the critics are one of the most important types of people in your life and if they stop talking, it means they gave up on you.

Since we each have our own personal perspectives about specific topics, many of us listen with the intent to *reply* back so we can express our opinions. It is much more challenging, but helpful, to listen with the intent of understanding the other person's point of view to learn from their message. If we can adopt the skill of listening to understand (rather than to reply), it can help us enhance our innovation in the long run because we can recognize what people like or dislike, but more importantly, *why* they feel this way.

Would you rather hear the truth from others or are you in fear the truth would destroy the illusion of your "perfect" reality? Would you rather be rewarded for what you've accomplished and then be done or not be rewarded and strive to accomplish more? Would you rather achieve in something average or fail in something extraordinary?

Due to natural instinct, many humans tend to focus on the negative characteristics of a person more than the positive. Therefore, sometimes when people can't achieve something themselves, they're going to say you can't do it as well. They will tear you apart, but it's your job to restore yourself; this time, more powerful than before.

There are three types of people who will say you cannot make a difference in the world: those who are afraid to try themselves and those who do not want you to succeed. The third? Yourself.

Name of Effect: "TnR (Torn and Restored)"
Advanced Napkin Trick

Basic Effect: The performer restores a ripped napkin.

What the Audience Sees: A paper napkin is torn into small pieces and squeezed between the spectator's hands. Then the performer slowly unravels the napkin to show the pieces weld themselves together again.

Background: This type of routine has gone down in magic books throughout the history of magic and has been a classic for all magicians. There are so many different and innovative ways you can perform this, but today I'll reveal the easiest one. You can perform this close up, on stage, or in the streets. When you know how to perform a trick that you can perform virtually anywhere, I highly suggest you practice it.

Method: First, you need two napkins. For explanation purposes, the pictures provided use two different colored napkins. However, when performing this trick, you need to use identical napkins (Figure 8.1 Exposed View).

Next, crumple one of them up and secretly place it in your hand. Try and hold this as natural and casual as possible so it looks like nothing is in your hand. Your setup is now complete (Figure 8.2 Exposed View) (Figure 8.3 Audience View).

Ask someone if they want to see a magic trick. When they say yes, pick up the second napkin and hold it flat with both hands (Figure 8.4 Audience View). Next, tear down the middle of the second napkin. This may take practice because (at the same time) you have to secretly hold the other napkin and can't let the audience see it.

Take the ripped pieces, bring them together, and tear them again. This time you should have four pieces. Tear all of those pieces so you have eight pieces now. Take those eight pieces and crumple them up into a ball (Figure 8.5 Audience View).

While you're rolling the pieces into a ball, switch the pieces of the napkin you just tore for the crumpled napkin you have hidden in your hand (Figure 8.6 Exposed View). You have to make sure that the torn pieces are "balled up" enough so it looks identical to the restored napkin in your hand.

As soon as you switched the torn pieces for the restored napkin, tell the audience you need to use your "magic wand." Reach down into your pocket with the torn pieces hidden in your hand, ditch the pieces in your pocket, and bring out a pencil, cell phone, or something to use as a "magic wand."

Have an audience member place their hand out and place the restored napkin in their hand. Next, ask the audience member to squeeze the "pieces of the napkin that you just ripped." Remember: the audience thinks what he or she is squeezing are pieces you just ripped (the audience member doesn't know the napkin is a completely different, restored napkin).

Next, use your "magic wand" and wave it over their hand (Figure 8.7 Audience View). Tell them to slowly open up their hand. You, the performer, should take the napkin out of their hand like the napkin is the most fragile thing in the world. Slowly open it up and reveal that the napkin restored itself!

Let's sum it up:

1. For your setup, get two identical napkins.

2. Take one of them, roll it up into a ball, and secretly palm it in your hand.

3. Next, ask the audience if they would like to see a trick.

4. Take the other napkin and spread it out as much as possible between both your hands.

5. Rip the napkin in half, then in fourths, then in eighths.

6. Crumple the pieces up into a ball.

7. Tell the audience you need to get your magic wand out of your pocket.

8. Keep the ball of the restored napkin in your right hand so the audience can see it as you secretly put the ball of pieces in your left hand while your reach for your wand.

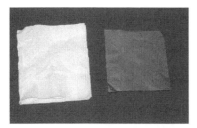

Figure 8.1 Exposed View

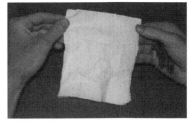

Figure 8.2 Exposed View

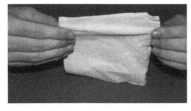

Figure 8.3 Audience View

Figure 8.4 Audience View

Figure 8.5 Audience View

Figure 8.6 Exposed View

Figure 8.7 Audience View

9. Ditch the pieces in your pocket and take out something "magical."

10. Place the restored napkin ball in the spectator's hand and ask him or her to close their hand as you wave the "wand" over it.

11. Slowly pick up the ball from the spectator's hand and unfold it carefully revealing it has restored back together!

Presentation Ideas/Alternate Methods/Tips:

"Pete, can I borrow your napkin for a second? I'll try a magic trick with it.

"I'll rip it a few times, but I'll show you that I can restore it with my magic wand....a glue stick! (At this point, ditch the missing pieces as you reach in your pocket to get the glue stick. If you use a glue stick as your "wand" people will laugh and they won't notice you ditched pieces of the napkin).

"But wait, hold on. I'll use the glue stick to restore them back to-gether, but I won't even open up the glue stick!

"Can you put your hand out for me? Squeeze the torn pieces as hard as you can. Okay, watch this. I'll wave my 'magical glue stick' over your hand. Open your hand up for me. As you can see, the pieces have been magically glued back together!"

When you reveal the restored napkin at the end, spread it out EXACTLY the same way you showed the first napkin. This image creates a certainty in the audience's mind that it is the same napkin you started out with. Also, when taking it out of the spectator's hand, handle the napkin very carefully as if it would break apart with ease. Remember: the audience thinks the napkin restored itself back together so you need to act as if the napkin is fragile.

One of the great advantages about this trick is if you use a bigger napkin or a newspaper (make sure the two pieces are identical), the trick will receive better reactions. But you have to make sure the audience members don't see the restored piece in your hand!

Also, make sure the ALWAYS sees one of the napkins the whole time. If your hands are completely covering both napkins, your audience will automatically think you switched the napkins....which you do, but in a very discreet manner. Good luck.

Nine.
Choices
-The Famous Envelope-

"In life you can only be young once, but you can be immature forever. So when you are trying to make a decision, if you do it you'll regret it, and if you don't do it, you'll also regret it. Therefore, either way you're going to regret it, so you might as well just do it. When you go to do it though, timing is everything because the early bird may get the worm, but the second mouse gets the cheese." -Thomas Chiarelli

Once we gather the criticism from others, we must not deny this advice; rather we must use it to our advantage. Over the years, we have become a society glued together by compliments, refusing to accept criticism and dismissing other opinions as ignorance instead of building a stronger foundation off of the advice. We can never please everyone in this world, but taking advice from an honest critic is one step closer in achieving what you want to accomplish. But it is our choice if we want to do this or not. And believe it or not, our choices not only impact us, but they impact society as a whole.

Let's take a step back for a moment. Humans are wired to receive and process information. From the information we receive, we interpret it based on what type of person we are. Wait a minute, what do you mean based on what type of person we are?

Through the years of performing and interacting with diverse audiences, I've come to the conclusion that there are two types of people in this world: the first type is "people-orientated" and the second type is "idea-orientated." When the "people-orientated" type are in a conversation, the main idea is about, well, people. For instance, what they are doing, what someone said, how someone feels, etc. These types of people will always bring the conversation back to themselves one way or another, either expressing their opinion internally or externally. The "idea-orientated" type, on the other hand, talk about ideas, objects, concepts, etc. Not sure which category you fall in? Next time you're in a conversation, consciously think about what you're saying back to the group or person. The words and thoughts you choose to express should answer that question for you.

Many of us decide on something based on what type of person we are. Regardless of which category you fall in, the important variable to emphasize is to not regret your decision. You wouldn't be able to determine the outcome if you didn't take the risk, correct? Instead of wondering whether or not you can do it, find out for sure. Give it a shot, but most of all, give it your best.

It could be minor, it could be substantial, but regardless your decisions impact the future of society. How? Well choices help build our lives. We are here right now based off a choice someone in the past made. And their choice was based off another choice. Therefore, everything you see around you, everything you perceive around you, is there from a choice made by someone. External influences impact us each day such as the clothes we wear, the places we go, the people we meet, the lessons we learn, the situations we're in, etc. Would you still be here right now if it weren't for your great-grandfather buying that ticket to sail overseas to meet your great-grandmother? Would you still hold moral values if you didn't listen to another person tell you their personal story on a specific subject? Would you still be able to read this sentence, if it weren't for your second grade teacher pursuing her passion for teaching? Therefore, without external influences, where would we be?

What if you had the ability to do *anything* you wanted to do without anyone knowing it was you? What would you do? Would you steal money to help your financial instability? Would you build something for the less fortunate? Or would you do something else? Even though the options are unlimited, the choices you make given this opportunity helps define your true character.

You may be content with your life at this very moment, but if you continue with your daily habitual routine right now, where do you see yourself in five years? If you're not satisfied with this picture, ask yourself what you can do differently with your life NOW in order to alter the potential outcome for your future.

Sometimes making choices can be easy, but what about taking risks? The courage we hold within ourselves can be a waste if we never truly show it. When taking any risk in life, we must understand that our actions can result in one out of two ways: it could be successful and benefit ourselves and others *or* it could evolve into an embarrassing failure story your family and friends never stop talking about.

Nonetheless, if we always take a ride down the comfortable, relaxed, and content road, our lives would be pretty boring and repetitive. Don't be hesitant to take a risk. You can do it, and if you don't, someone else will, and you may regret not stepping up. We all know that taking risks can be scary at times, but imagine if no one took any. What would society look like?

Name of Effect: "The Famous Envelope"
Intermediate Mind Trick

Basic Effect: The performer predicts the card the audience will cut to.

What the Audience Sees: An envelope is shown by the performer and put to the side. The performer shows the cards are all different and hands the deck to any audience member to have them shuffle. Once the audience member is satisfied with the mix, the deck is placed on the table. Another audience member is called up on stage to freely cut the cards wherever he or she wants. The performer puts an envelope on the card the audience member cut to, to mark the spot. The performer lets the audience member look at the selected card that he or she cut to. Finally, the performer lets the audience member open up the envelope- the prediction matches.

The Famous Envelope

Background: It does require a little setup beforehand, but man oh man this effect is beautiful. From the audience's point of view, you knew exactly what card someone would cut to after the deck has been shuffled. Keep in mind that the performer never touches the deck!

Method: Before you begin, take out a random card from the deck and place it to the side. For explanation purposes, let's use the nine of spades (Figure 9.1 Exposed View). Next, you need a small envelope and write "Prediction" on the front of it. After that, take a sticky note and write "Nine of Spades" on it (Figure 9.2 Exposed View). Place the sticky note inside the envelope and seal it.

Once this is complete, hold the nine of spades behind the envelope. To the audience, it should look like the envelope is the only thing in your hand. You are now done with the setup (Figure 9.3 Audience View) (Figure 9.4 Exposed View).

As soon as you're ready to perform, ask an audience member to come on stage and to verify all of the cards in the deck are different. Then, politely ask him or her to shuffle the deck as much as they want (the deck has all of the cards in it except for the nine of spades). As they are doing this, explain to the rest of your audience you wrote down a prediction and it is sealed inside the envelope you are holding (while saying this, you are also secretly holding the nine of spades behind the envelope).

Once they are satisfied with the shuffle, he or she should place the deck on the table. Ask the same spectator, or a different one, to pick up the deck wherever he or she wants and to place that half on the table next to the first half (have an audience member cut the deck) (Figure 9.5 Audience View).

Explain to your audience you will mark where the cards were cut with your "prediction" envelope. All you need to do is place the envelope on the card the audience cut to. As you probably realized by now, if you place the envelope on top of the pile the spectator cut to, the nine of spades will now be the top card of the pile (Figure 9.6 Exposed View).

DELAY some time by explaining that they shuffled the deck and they cut wherever they wanted. Then, ask him or her to pick up the envelope and place it to the side. Finally, ask your audience member

77

Figure 9.1 Exposed View

Figure 9.2 Exposed View

Figure 9.3 Audience View

Figure 9.4 Exposed View

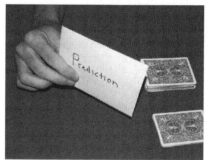

Figure 9.5 Audience View

Figure 9.6 Exposed View

Figure 9.7
Audience View

to take the card they cut to (of course this is not their card, but they think it is). As he or she flips over the so-called "cut card," the audience will think the card that was cut to was the nine of spades. Have another audience member open up the envelope revealing the prediction! (Figure 9.7 Audience View).

Let's sum it up:

1. Take out a random card from the pile of the deck and write this card down on a sticky note.

2. Place the sticky note inside the envelope labeled "Prediction" and hold the selected card behind the envelope out of sight from the audience.

3. When you're ready to perform, show the cards are different and have an audience member shuffle the deck up as much as he or she wants.

4. Have an audience member cut the cards wherever he or she wants.

5. Place the envelope on top of the pile the audience member cut to as a place mark to where the cut was.

6. Delay some time by explaining to your audience the deck consists of different cards, it was thoroughly mixed, and then cut to a random spot.

7. Have an audience member lift up the envelope and place it to the side, looking at the "cut to" card. Open up the envelope and reveal the prediction!

Presentation Ideas/Alternate Methods/Tips:

As I mentioned, you want to delay time between placing the envelope on the pile the audience member cut to and the end reveal. I suggest you distract the audience somehow for approximately ten seconds before you have someone lift up the envelope from the cards. In order for the audience to believe that the envelope has nothing to do with the trick, this needs to be done.

One example is to ask what the audience member's name is and you apologize for not asking in the beginning. All you need is three or four seconds for the audience to get their mind off the trick. After I change the subject for a short amount of time, I come back and usually re-cap before I reveal the prediction.

In addition, try not to go near the deck as much as possible. This trick is all about the audience and their freedom so the more you're not interfering with that, the better shape you'll be in. The only time you should be near the deck is when you place the envelope down as you load the prediction card. Good luck.

Ten.
Self-Belief
-Impossible Three-

"It really is a crazy world out there. Everything that is meant to happen will happen. And if this rule is broken, well, then you got yourself a case of magic." -David DuVal

After we have recognized that every choice we make cannot only impact ourselves, but also the future of society, we must take into consideration that self-belief is also a choice. Unfortunately, society has taught most of us that if we do not achieve something, we should often immediately and characterize it as an impossible task; the illusion of self-belief, resulting in self-defeat.

What is self-belief to begin with? It's simply the ability to believe you will accomplish a specific task no matter what obstacles stand in the way. Without self-belief we have no self-confidence. Without self-confidence we are less effective in whatever we do. But self-confidence is a skill. Just like with any other skill in life, in order to be proficient, we must practice. When you have a goal or challenge in life, you need to approach it with the attitude of *"**When** I accomplish this, then xyz"* rather than *"**If** I accomplish this, then xyz."*

Many people think they reserved a small spot in their brain expecting self-confidence to "magically" appear one day. Contrary to popular belief, that's not the formula for success. Repetition and persistence, along with the belief that you possess the required skills, is what helps you grow confident and competent at what you do. The more you practice self-belief, the more you will enhance your self-confidence. In return, you'll be able to produce higher quality results in any task you perform in life.

For example, according to scientists, humans and monkeys share 98% of their DNA. The most intellectually advanced humans can send satellites into space, perform triple bypass biopsy's on patients, interpret the laws of quantum physics, and so on. Our most advanced monkeys are lucky if they can draw a stick figure or pronounce a small set of syllables for a banana.

So what does two percent really mean? Two percent isn't as small as most people think it is. You may think at times you are giving your full effort, but do you have the ability to give two percent more? And, if you do, how big of a difference could that make? Understand that giving an extra two percent could potentially result in achieving your own personal goals. However, there is another way as well: looking at the situation from a different perspective.

Right now think of a goal you want to achieve in your life. You may think it's impossible to do, but sometimes it's not. Why? Well, if you just witnessed a performance (or magic trick) of something impossible become possible, and you have a specific goal in your life you want to achieve, but you think it's impossible to do, wouldn't you be contradicting yourself? After experiencing magic, you should try to set higher standards for yourself and reconsider what your true potential in life is. Sometimes all we need is a paradigm shift to motivate ourselves.

When someone says that you cannot achieve something, remember they are most likely speaking from within the boundaries of their own limits and past experiences. If you stop exploring, no matter what it is, what does that say about you? If you take that forward, what does it say about your attitude? Since so much of the world remains a mystery, how can we rule out possibilities?

It's very "human" of us to want to cling to the little bits of truth we're sure of, but we can't let these facts prevent us from finding our true potential. If every person in the world understood this concept, imagine what society could accomplish. Let me rephrase that: if *impossible* is just a word, what can *you* accomplish?

Name of Effect: "Impossible Three"
Beginner Mind Trick

Basic Effect: The audience member writes down three different words on three different notecards, respectively, and thinks of one without telling anyone else. The performer can instantly reveal the word they are thinking of.

What the Audience Sees: The performer takes out three blank notecards. He asks the audience member to think of three different animals. On each notecard, the performer (or spectator) writes down a different animal, resulting in three different animals. The performer asks the audience member to think of one while the performer turns his back. After the audience member thinks of an animal, the audience member flips over the notecards so they are face down. Next, the audience member switches the position of the two animals that he or she didn't think of, leaving the selected animal in the same spot. Once the performer turns back around, the notecards are still face down so the performer doesn't know the location of any of the animals. Another audience member mixes up the face down notecards even more. The notecards are turned face up again and the performer instantly reveals the selection.

Background: In the eyes of the audience, you are truly reading their mind. Plus, you can do this anytime and anywhere as this is strong magic at its best.

Method: First, have the audience think of three random things. In this case, using animals are easy so we'll use a dog, a tiger, and an elephant. To make it more entertaining you could have people draw these animals on the notecards.

Next, place the notecards in a row and tell your audience member to think of one. At this point, all you are going to do is remember the MIDDLE animal. For explanation purposes, let's use the tiger as the middle animal (Figure 10.1 Audience View).

Once you've memorized the middle animal, turn your back and tell the audience to switch the positions of the two animals they *didn't* think of. For explanation purposes, let's say the audience member thought of the elephant. So, in this case, he or she would switch the positions of the tiger and the dog (Figure 10.2 Audience View).

Then, have the audience member flip over all of the cards so they are face DOWN. Remember: your back is turned when they do all of this so you don't know what their selection is.

When you turn back around, keep your eye on the middle card and repeat the word "tiger" in your head (because it was the original middle card). Then, YOU mix up the cards even more. Once again, all you're doing is keeping your eye on the middle card and repeating the word "tiger" in your head. Remember: the cards are face DOWN while you're doing this (Figure 10.3 Audience View).

After you mix the cards up even more (let's say five seconds of mixing), you can turn over the cards so they are face up. Below are the future outcomes (the following circumstances would only be true if the original middle card was the tiger):

Option 1: If the card you were keeping track of is STILL the original middle card, in this case the tiger, then the audience member was thinking of the tiger.

Option 2: If the card you were keeping track of is the dog, then the audience member was thinking of the elephant.

Option 3: If the card you were keeping track of is the elephant, then the audience member was thinking of the dog.

Let's sum it up:

1. Write three different animals on three different notecards.

2. Memorize what the middle animal is.

3. Turn your back and tell your audience member to think of a card with one of the animals on it.

4. Tell them to swap the positions of the two cards they are NOT

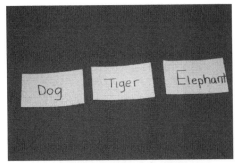

Figure 10.1 Audience View

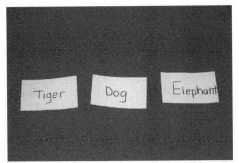

Figure 10.2 Audience View

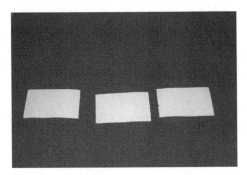

Figure 10.3 Audience View

thinking of, therefore leaving the animal they ARE thinking of in the same spot.

5. Tell your audience to turn the cards face down so when you turn back around you don't know the location of each animal.

6. Turn back around.

7. Have another audience member (or yourself) mix up the cards as well, but make sure YOU secretly keep your eye on the middle card.

8. Have the audience member flip over the cards so they are face up again.

9. If the card you kept your eye on is STILL the ORIGINAL middle card (the animal you memorized in the beginning), then that IS the animal the audience thought of.

10. If the card you kept your eye on is NOT the animal you memorized in the beginning, it is NOT the animal you memorized in the beginning NOR the animal that is on the card; therefore, it is the OTHER animal (card).

Presentation Ideas/Alternate Methods/Tips:

"Hey Bart, I have three blank notecards here. I need you to think of any three animals you want. A dog, tiger, and elephant? Perfect. I'll write them down and lay them horizontally just like this (memorize the middle card).

"I'll turn my back so I can't see what you're doing. What I need you to do is think of one of the animals. Once you got one, let me know. Perfect.

"Please switch positions of the two animals you aren't thinking of, so the animal you are thinking of stays in the same location. Let me know when you've done that.

"I'm going to turn back around in a second so please flip the cards face down so I don't know where they are. Ready? (Turn back around, keep your eye on the middle card, and repeat tiger in your head since that was the original middle card).

"Now I'll mix them up even more so hopefully you won't know where your selected animal is (mix the cards up fast but make sure to keep your eye on the middle card).

"I'll flip them face up now so we know where the animals are. Okay, okay, based off my mental ability, I'm going to say you were thinking of an elephant."

Something VERY important to keep in mind: once you turn back around, you need the cards to be mixed up again. I usually like to mix them up myself really fast so most people can't keep their eye on their card, but you can have someone else do it as well. You just need to make sure you know where the middle card is. If you don't mix them up a second time, many people will think you just memorized the order of the three cards. In a sense you did, but with a sneaky method.

If you're confused by the method at first, just try it on yourself and it should work. I know I told you in the beginning of this book to never perform a trick more than once to the same audience, but I highly doubt they will figure this method out. In fact, it will probably make them more frustrated (in a good way) if you perform it more than once!

Rather than using animals, you can use different playing cards instead. Or if you want to be really creative, you can have someone draw your group of friends. This will always get a good laugh and then you can make up a funny plot to go along with the trick (in addition to criticizing their drawing skills of you). Good luck.

Eleven.
Success
-ascib-

"Honesty, hard work, dedication, and respect for your family and neighbors is what builds a strong world. When these things are lacking, it leads to lack of trust and deception, as well as financial ruin. We need a strong world today." -Jim Sylvia

What does it mean to be successful? Is it based on the truth? What society tells us? Our own inner truth? *Success.* Such an incredible, powerful, yet arbitrary word. Once we have a proficient skill set in our self-belief and self-confidence, we can then determine what "success" means to us personally.

Sometimes it seems that society is forcing us to run in a race toward success, but no one knows where the finish line is. One of the most depressing things in life is watching someone work hard at something, but not succeed in the way he or she expected, or in a way that is not rewarded by society.

What if there was a button you could push at any moment that could make your dreams and life goals instantly come true? Would you push it if you had the opportunity? Or would you rather experience the obstacles, hardships, and stress on the way as you attempt to achieve your goals?

What would you do if money didn't matter? Think about it. If there was no such thing as money, how would you really enjoy spending your own individual time? When you finally find something that you really want to do, forget the money. If you say that earning money is the most important thing in your life, you will be wasting your life doing things you don't necessarily enjoy doing (just because money is the end result).

There are many different paths to success and many different ways to define success. Does success mean having an academic degree? Does success mean having a viral video? Does success mean having money? Or does success mean spending your life in your own way? What about you? Do you think you're successful?

Name of Effect: "Anytime Signed Coin in Bottle/a.s.c.i.b."
Advanced Coin Trick

Basic Effect: A signed coin penetrates through a empty plastic water bottle.

What the Audience Sees: A signed coin and an empty plastic water bottle are borrowed from an audience member. The performer shows the audience there are no holes in the bottle on all sides. With his sleeves rolled up and the signed coin in his palm, the performer slams the coin on the side of the bottle and the coin visually travels through the plastic and into the bottle. Everything is examinable.

Background: The effect is based off of Matthew Mello's "Bullet" and Gier Bratiles's "Infusion." Inspired by both ideas, I created what you are about to learn. However, the first thing that people will think if you "slam" a coin through a bottle is there are either duplicate coins or there are holes in the bottle. These two ideas are instantly eliminated with this method, leaving people more astonished.

Method: First, borrow a coin (using a quarter or a nickel works best with this) and an empty Gatorade or Vitamin bottle. Have the spectator sign the coin and ask them to hold it for a second. Next, take the bottle and place it horizontally so the cap of the bottle is in your right palm. Take your left hand and grab the bottle from the bottom. Use

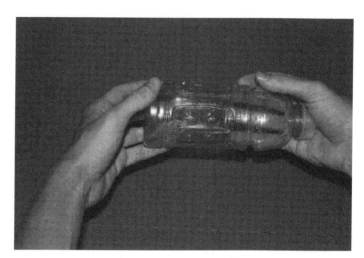

Figure 11.1 Exposed View

your right thumb muscle from your palm for a spot to place the cap. Start turning the bottle towards the audience as you want them to notice there are no holes or slits within the bottle (Figure 11.1 Exposed View).

What you are actually doing here is killing two birds with one stone. If you try this now, you'll realize the cap is becoming looser. Once it is loose enough, the cap should snuggle into your right palm. With your fingers concealing the top of the bottle, notice that if you take the bottle with your left hand and move it slightly to the left (pulling away), you can separate the cap and the bottle (Figure 11.2 Exposed View).

The spectators shouldn't notice this because you'll be explaining there are no holes in the bottle and your right hand will be covering the maneuver. Next, take your left hand off the bottle, but turn the bottle slightly toward the audience. As a result, the bottle isn't directly parallel with the cap anymore, which is in your right hand (Figure 11.3 Exposed View).

Take the signed coin and place it in your left palm. Since the cap is snuggled in your right hand, as long as you don't release tension from your fingers, the cap shouldn't fall out. As a result, the coin should be in your left palm, the bottom of the bottle should be slanted a little towards the audience, and the cap of the bottle should be in your right palm while the right hand is holding the bottle as well (Figure 11.4 Exposed View).

What you are about to do may take practice so don't be discouraged if you can't do it the first time you try. Since you're holding the bottle with your right hand, tap the side of the bottle a few times against the coin, which is flat in your left hand. Explain to the audience there is no way the coin could travel through the bottle. Each time you tap the bottle with the coin, try and make it faster and faster. On the last time you tap the coin, slant the bottle up just a little. When you come down to slam the coin with the bottle, scoop the coin into the mouth of the bottle (Figure 11.5 Exposed View).

If done correctly, it will look like the coin traveled through the bottle. Wait, how do you get the cap back on? Restate there are no holes! The audience will be reacting by this point, so you just need to take advantage of it. Spin the bottle again, but faster this time and in the

Figure 11.2 Exposed View

Figure 11.3 Exposed View

Figure 11.4 Exposed View

Figure 11.5 Exposed View

opposite direction. While you're doing this, explain there couldn't be any possible way the coin could have gone through the bottle. Once the cap is back on you can immediately give everything out for examination.

Let's sum it up:

1. Have the spectator sign the coin.

2. Hold the bottle horizontally with the cap facing your right hand.

3. Spin the bottle with your left hand towards the audience as the cap becomes palmed in your right hand.

4. Once the cap is completely off, take the coin and place it flat in your left hand.

5. Use the bottle in your right hand and tap the coin a few times.

6. On the last tap, scoop the coin from your left hand into the opening of the bottle.

7. As the audience is reacting, quickly turn the bottle the opposite way so the cap goes back on (or simply pretend you're taking the cap off).

Presentation Ideas/Alternate Methods/Tips:

"Do you have a coin on you? Great. Now I need you to sign it so there's no way I can duplicate it.

"May I borrow your Gatorade bottle for a second? I want you to notice there is nothing in the bottle. Additionally, notice there are no holes (palm cap while turning bottle).

"If I place your signed coin in my left hand like this, you'll see something strange. If I hit the coin a few times on the bottle....SLAM.

"Look, the coin is INSIDE the bottle now. I'll show you again there are no holes (turn bottle opposite way so the cap goes back on). Check it out for yourself!"

Instead of scooping the coin, it might be easier to drop your left hand very fast, leaving the coin suspended in mid-air for a brief second allowing you to grab the coin with the bottle (both methods work for me).

Also, it's not necessary to put a lot of effort in screwing the cap back on. You can easily put your palm on the top of the bottle once the coin is in the bottle. In this case, place the cap back on top and pretend to just screw it off. The audience will be reacting anyway so it won't really matter, as long as they see the cap is on the top. You can then immediately dump the signed coin into the spectator's hand.

The hard part of the trick will be getting the coin in the mouth of the bottle. The timing on that move needs to be flawless and should take no longer than two seconds.

If you use the correct size cap, it should fit perfectly in your palm. Regular water bottles normally don't work so I would just stick with Gatorade or Vitamin water bottles. It's a nice little routine after a workout! Good luck.

Twelve.
Identity
-The Lipstick Trick-

"Everything will be okay. Think about what happened a year ago today. You probably can't remember, huh? Everything that seems important now won't be any more after time. Things find a way of working themselves out, and are never as impossible as they seem. Don't think about how hard everything seems to always be for you, because there's always someone that has it worse. You have two moving feet and a beating heart. Use your feet and go find someone or something that makes your heart happy. Whatever happens is supposed to happen. I can't promise you it will work out the way that you had hoped, but there is no reason to believe everything won't work out in the end. Fight for what you believe in, and always listen to your heart."
-Emily Tiedtke

So you now have your own definition of "success" and what it truly means to you. But in the modern world today, how "successful" you are usually correlates to your "identity" to some degree. As a result, titles tend to define people in life. Sometimes it's a good thing, yet other times people can take them too seriously. They may go after opportunities that would help them receive a higher "title" in the community, but it's not exactly what they truly want.

It's easy to take a step off the path and make your own, but you have to make sure this path is heading towards the same direction of who you are and what you want to become. Having a loftier title than another person does not mean you are better. It is your job to put a definition behind your *own* title and create the experience that really matters to *you.*

For instance, I wrote this entire book before I figured out the title. Well, let me rephrase that: I wrote this entire book, except for this chapter, before I figured out the title. To have one phrase, only a few words, representing everything in this book, is a hard thing to do.

At first I wanted to think of something original, unique, and special. I wanted to think of something that would catch the eye at first glance. I wanted to think of something innovative enough that Shakespeare would bring me out to lunch.

Until one day, the title you read now magically popped into my head. It was like God tapped me on the shoulder, whispered in my ear and said, "Stop thinking too much. You are trying to sound smarter than you actually are." It was then I realized the titles I was battling between had nothing to do with what this book is actually about. Soon afterwards I understood that the title is one of the most important factors in writing a book. Not only does the title create curiosity to the reader, but it also brings a title to who I am as a person and as an author.

But that's enough about me. Without using your name, *who are you?* How do you define yourself? You might answer this question by describing physical traits or explaining hobbies and activities you enjoy. Or perhaps you would talk about specific titles you hold in the community. But deep down, behind what is seen from the naked eye, who are you really? The only person who truly knows the answer to this question is **you.** Not your family members. Not your best friends. Not your colleagues. YOU.

Before you go to sleep at night, you lay in bed and reflect on your day, predict the events for tomorrow, and analyze your anxieties. It is this moment when you truly know who you are. This is when each and every one of us takes off our masks and realize how transparent these masks really are. Because honestly, the thickness of our masks symbolizes the boundary that separates who we really are and the perception others have of us; the illusion of identity.

Name of Effect: "The Lipstick Trick"
Advanced Miscellaneous Trick

Basic Effect: A dot of lipstick appears on a spectator's hand without the performer touching the spectator.

What the Audience Sees: A performer asks for some lipstick and the spectator makes a fist with one of his or her hands. A dot of lipstick is put on the performer's hand and then the performer starts rubbing it off. Once the dot of lipstick has rubbed off the performer's hand, the spectator opens his or her hand and the dot of lipstick travelled from the performer's hand to the spectator's hand!

Background: When I first saw this performed I thought there was some type of video editing. When I started to understand the method, I was surprised how simple it was. Soon enough, I started to perform the trick and it baffled so many people! With such a simple method, but hard hitting impact, most of your audience members will turn their heads in confusion.

Method: Ask someone if they have any lipstick with them. Once they hand you the lipstick, open it, look at it confused, and say "We actually need two. Does anyone in the audience have another one?" Although you are completely lying to them, this is where the secret move comes in. As people look around, secretly put some lipstick on your middle finger with the opposite hand of the one you're holding the lipstick with. From the audience point of view, it looks like you're just placing your hands together. If you do this move naturally, no one will be paying attention to you (everyone will be looking for the second lipstick anyway!) (Figure 12.1 Exposed View)

Your setup is complete. Once you put a little lipstick on your finger, wait five more seconds with the chaos of everyone looking for lipstick and say "Actually, this is fine. I've never done the trick with one type of lipstick before, so I guess this will be new for you *and* me."

Ask the person who handed you the lipstick to place both their hands out palms down. Under your breath (like you're talking to yourself), say "Just a little higher." As you're saying this, raise both their hands up, using your thumbs and middle fingers. If done correctly, the lipstick that was on your middle finger in the beginning is now imprinted on one of their palms (Figure 12.2 Exposed View).

Next, ask the audience member if he or she is right-handed or left-handed. For explanation purposes, let's say you put the lipstick on YOUR LEFT middle finger in the beginning. As a result, the lipstick should be on THEIR RIGHT palm. So, in this case, if the audience member is a right-handed person, you need to tell him or her to close their right hand into a fist and put their left hand to the side. If the audience member is a left-handed person, you need to tell him or her that since they are left-handed, he or she should put their left hand to the side and that you'll use their right hand instead. No matter what they say, the end result is the same (just make sure that whatever hand they have the lipstick on is the same hand that stays out).

After the audience member has their hand closed with the lipstick on their palm (which they don't know about), put the stick of lipstick in your hand that has the mark on your middle finger, in this case, the LEFT hand. Next, make a fist with your right hand. Take the lipstick in your left hand and put a dot on the BACK of your right hand so everyone can see (Figure 12.3 Audience View).

Put your right fist over the fist of the audience member. Take your left hand (which has the lipstick mark on your middle finger) and rub the lipstick on your right hand until the majority of it on the back of your palm starts to rub away. Have the audience member check their hand! (Figure 12.4 Audience View).

Let's sum it up:

1. Ask for some lipstick and after you receive one, ask for another one.

2. As people are searching for a second type of lipstick, secretly place some on your middle finger (try to do this without looking).

3. Tell the audience you will try to perform with one lipstick instead of two this time.

4. Ask someone to place both their hands out straight.

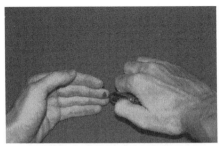

Figure 12.1 Exposed View

Figure 12.2 Exposed View

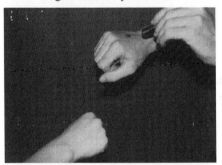

Figure 12.3 Audience View

Figure 12.4 Audience View

5. Under your breath, naturally say "just a little higher." As you do this, use your middle finger and thumb to raise both their hands.

6. Ask the audience member if they are right handed or left handed and to make a fist (use your presentation to eliminate the correct hand).

7. Use your hand to make a fist (the hand that doesn't have the lipstick on the finger).

8. Put a dot of lipstick on the back of your fist and rub it in with the opposite hand (that already has the lipstick on the finger from the beginning).

9. Once the majority of it has vanished, ask the audience member to open up their fist. It will seem the lipstick has travelled from your hand to the spectator's hand!

Presentation Ideas/Alternate Methods/Tips

"Hi everyone, I'm going to try something tonight with an object I normally don't use. Does anyone have any lipstick? Great, thanks Simon, you're the best. Don't worry, I won't tell your girlfriend.

"We actually need a second one as well. Does anyone have another one? (apply lipstick to your finger and wait five seconds). Never mind, we can just use one for now. I've never done the trick with one type before so bear with me if it doesn't work.

"Simon, could you place both your hands out for me. Just a little higher, perfect. Are you right-handed or left-handed? You're left-handed? Okay, this works out perfect. Can you remove your left hand and form a fist with your right hand?

"I'll do the same thing with my hand. Now I'll take the lipstick and put a dot on the back of my hand. If I place my fist over your fist, you might feel something strange. I'll rub the lipstick away with my hand

and it looks like the dot is disappearing. To be honest, the dot is actually teleporting. Don't believe me? Open up your fist and take a look!"

Hold your horses Mr. Logan, what happens if people bring out more than one lipstick at the same time? All you need to do is take one, ask another person to put their lipstick away, and then after a few seconds ask if you can borrow the second one again, do your move and then disregard it again. This will get a good laugh because from the audience point of view, it seems like you can't make up your mind, yet you do the secret move.

Many people may ask you afterwards "What would happen if you used two lipsticks?" Well, in order to avoid that conversation, you can incorporate it within your presentation. For instance, after the lipstick rubs off your hand, you could turn over your hand and say "Hmm... normally it travels to my palm (flip over your hand and act confused why it's not there). Wait a minute, since we only used one lipstick this time, I'm curious if it travelled somewhere else. Can you flip over *your* hand for me?"

Another thing to keep in mind is NOT to expose the lipstick on your finger. Try to naturally bend the hand that has the lipstick on the middle finger. When you finally touch the person, make sure it's subtle enough so when the audience member looks back on the trick, he or she will have no flashbacks whatsoever of you touching them at any point. In other words, don't apply a lot of pressure to their hand (you don't need a lot of lipstick on your finger to begin with either). Instead, just raise both their hands as you normally would because the trick is still impressive even if a little lipstick appears on their hand without them knowing how it got there.

The majority of girls have lipstick in their purse, so this trick is a perfect way to impress the chicks- anywhere at anytime. You could even say that their lips must be magical because their lipstick is magical! Actually, that might not be a good idea. Good luck.

Thirteen.
Halftime
-Crayon-

"If the rain keeps up, it won't come down." -Chris Taylor

So far you've identified your passions, received criticism based off your work, and understood who you were by enhancing your self-confidence and creating your own definition of "success" (just to name a few). People who work hard like this deserve a break. So let's take one!

Go on a bike ride and then make yourself a nice peanut butter and jelly sandwich with some chocolate milk on the side...unless you're allergic to nuts. I can't be held liable for any type of allergic reactions to food suggestions. Anyway, I'm in the mood to go on a run. I'll probably take a nap afterwards though. Adiós.

Name of Effect: "Crayon"
Beginner Mind Trick

Basic Effect: The performer knows the color of the crayon the audience is thinking of.

What the Audience Sees: The audience member takes out any colored crayon from a crayon box while the performer's back is turned. The audience member places the crayon in the performer's hand. As the performer turns back around, he can reveal the color of the crayon the audience member chose.

Background: This is perfect for restaurants, especially with the kids menu. I'm not really sure who the creator is, but nonetheless, it's quick, easy, and any level performer can perform it!

Method: Ask an audience member to choose any colored crayon as you turn your back. When they finally choose one, have them place it into your hand and they should take away the rest of the crayons on the table (Figure 13.1 Audience View).

When you turn your body back around, the crayon is still in your hand, but your hand is behind you (away from the audience). As you turn around to face the audience, take the crayon that's behind your back and color some of it on your fingernail. This should take no more than three seconds (Figure 13.2 Exposed View).

Next, bring the hand that's been colored on out from behind your back, but keep the hand that has the crayon in it behind your back. Bring the hand with the crayon on the fingernail up to chest level and have the audience stare into your palm. At this point, you want to tell your audience to imagine the color of the crayon on your palm. As you do this, just look at your fingernail and see what color the crayon is. Once you know what the color is, reveal the color to your audience with any approach you want. After you reveal the color, you can bring the crayon out from behind your back to confirm with your audience you were correct.

Let's sum it up:

1. Turn your back and have an audience member place any colored crayon in your hand (ask them to take the other crayons off the table as well after they place the crayon in your hand).

2. Turn back around, but keep the crayon behind your back.

3. Quickly color your fingernail with the crayon behind your back.

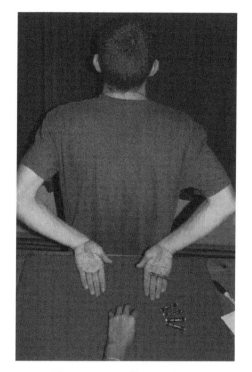

Figure 13.1 Audience View

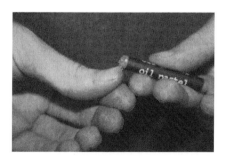

Figure 13.2 Exposed View

4. Bring out the hand that is colored and tell the audience to stare into your palm and picture the color on your palm while you look at your fingernail to reveal the color.

Presentation Ideas/Alternate Methods/Tips:

"Hey Phil, I have a box of crayons here. As you can see, there are over 20 different colors. What I need you to do is look through the box and pick any color you want. I'll turn my back and let me know when you're done.

"Once you selected a color, please place the crayon in my hand and take the other crayons off the table. Perfect.

"As I turn back around, I want you to picture the color of the crayon in your mind (quickly apply to fingernail). If it makes it easier, I'll have you stare into my palm (bring out hand and have your palm face them as you realize what the color is). Okay, okay, I'm sensing it's a short word. My palm is heating up right now. Are you thinking of the color red?"

If you angle yourself correctly, the audience shouldn't see anything on your fingernail. Once you reveal the color, you can give the crayon back and wipe the color off with your hand. Other than the fun games and good food, this is another reason why I still order off the kids menu. Good luck.

Fourteen.
Time
-Prisoner-

"Be strong. So many things in the world try and break you, but you have to be better than all of that and overcome the obstacles. You need to be the change, and be that better person everybody is looking for. But don't be somebody for them. Just do the right thing and don't look for attention from it." -Amanda Parry

You're now in retirement. This is the part of your life where you start to reflect on specific moments and Time can either be your friend or foe. Nonetheless, we can never have full control over his illusion as he is a mysterious thief who never seems to die out.

Imagine someone has been filming your entire life. You now have the ability to fast forward different phases you went through. You now have the ability to pause specific moments and react to them. You now have the ability to rewind and realize how different your life could have been if you made a different decision. All of the happiness, contentment, pleasure, depression, anger, and confusion could be at your fingertips. Are you ready for all of your emotions to be controlled with a button? We all have a story to share. Is yours worth watching?

We tend to spend more time dreaming of the future, not realizing that a little of it slips away every day. Most of us never take into consideration that what is happening to us now has also happened to others before. When we are young, we act as if we are the first young people in the world and tend to believe we can live forever.

In reality, we must confess that when we say the word "forever," we have to take into consideration that this "forever" concept is only composed of the "nows" we live in. In other words, the future and past only exist in our minds. We make plans for the future, we invoke memories of our past, but what is important is this very moment. Like it or not, we are all partners in this dull, mundane, but unpredictable moment. That's the beauty of it all; our world, an unwrapped present under the tree full of possibilities. Maybe we've had times in the past that were special for us, and maybe the future will hold priceless moments as well, but the only time we truly possess is right now. And what we do with this time is ours to decide.

Name of Effect: "Prisoner"
Beginner Card Trick

Basic Effect: A prediction card that has been written down is the only card that stays in a cup after the other cards have fallen out.

What the Audience Sees: A prediction is written down after the audience shuffles the deck. A cup is then held upside down and the deck of cards is placed in the cup tight enough so the cards won't fall out. Someone shakes the cup side-to-side which gives enough momentum so the cards from the cup scatter everywhere. Soon enough, all of the cards come out of the cup except for one card. The prediction is flipped over and it matches the card that stayed in the cup.

Background: I was fifteen years old at the time and I already created "Black Hole" a few days prior. As a result, I had the mindset of using a cup or glass in order to accomplish a trick. I went to my cabinet and found a tall plastic see-through cup and noticed how the majority of cups go inwards at the bottom. I started playing around and finally thought of this simple and neat trick.

The next day was a Friday and we ran a road race at our school (Fun fact: the author of this book finished first overall in the race).

Since it was a weekend, my buddy asked if I wanted to head back to his house and spend the night. We were watching television until his brother came in the room and I took this as an opportunity to perform my new trick. Surprisingly, the reaction was absolutely priceless since their parents came downstairs wondering what the commotion was all about.

Method: What you need is a tall plastic cup or glass (I'll refer to a cup for explanation purposes). The cup also needs to start out fat at the top and slowly get skinnier once it reaches the bottom so when you place a deck of cards in there, the cards will get stuck if you hold the cup upside down. But also make sure there is enough room so that the cards can get stuck in the cup *without* reaching the bottom.

Next, have an audience member shuffle the deck. Take the deck back and tell the audience you will make a prediction. Fan through the deck to yourself (make sure no one else sees the cards), but only memorize the top card. You want to tell the audience you're making a prediction, however don't just look at the top card and write it down (performing magic is all about acting, so spread through the EN-TIRE deck). You could even pretend to struggle deciding what card you should write down (have this process take about seven seconds) (Figure 14.1 Exposed View)

Gather the deck, write down the top card, and flip the piece of paper upside down so no one can see it. Tell your audience this is your prediction. Take the deck and stick it in the cup until the cards become stuck (for instance, when the cup is upside down none of the cards should fall out). Turn the cup around so the top of the deck is facing you and the bottom card is facing the audience.

Take your right hand and hold the cup so your forefingers are in front and your thumb is in back. There should also be a gap between the bottom of the cup and the cards. Make sure your fingers cover this gap because this is where the secret move comes in (Figure 14.2 Exposed View).

While you are pushing the cards in, take your left hand and push the top card up a little more than the other cards (this can be done using your left thumb), but don't move the card up so much that it's noticeable. The audience won't see the card anyway because your

Figure 14.1 Exposed View

Figure 14.2 Exposed View

right hand will be covering the gap (Figure 14.3 Exposed View).

Right now you should have the cup held upside down with the cards stuck inside and the top card should be pushed up a little more than the other cards. Your hand is in front of the cup so your fingers are covering the gap between the cards and the bottom of the cup, thus covering the revelation of the prediction card which is pushed up more.

You are now done with the technical part of the trick. Take your right hand and shake the cup with the cards in it. Hold the cup with the cards in front of you and only move your wrist back and forth. If you do this fast enough, cards will scatter out of the cup. As a result, their card will always stay in there because you pushed it up more than the other cards (Figure 14.4 Audience View).

Let's sum it up:

1. Have a person shuffle the cards.

2. Take the deck back and look through the entire deck by yourself while telling your audience you will write down a prediction.

3. Write down the top card.

4. Place the deck in a tall cup or glass that gets skinnier towards the bottom.

5. Have the top of the deck face you and the bottom of the deck face the audience.

6. Using your hand, cover the gap between the cards and the bottom of the glass.

7. With the opposite hand, push the cards in even more, but push the top card up significantly more than the others.

8. Shake the deck and the top card should stay in there while the other cards scatter in the air.

Figure 14.3 Exposed View

Figure 14.4 Audience View

Presentation Ideas/Alternate Methods/Tips:

"Andrew, I have a deck of cards here and I need you to shuffle them as much as you want. That's perfect.

"I'm going to look through the deck and write down a prediction (fan through the deck for about seven seconds and write down the top card).

"I'll place the prediction face down here so no one can see it. This prediction will be here the entire time and I won't touch it.

"The deck will be placed in the cup. I'll push the cards in the cup deep enough so when I flip the cup upside down, they become stuck (cover the gap with the hand you're holding the cup with and use the opposite hand to push the top card up more).

"I would back up if I were you. I'll take the cup, shake it, and as you can see, cards fly everywhere.

"But look, one card stayed in there. You can flip over my prediction now- perfect match."

This trick is really easy to perform and is perfect for a party setting. Although it's an easy trick, if you apply some kick-ass presentation, your audience will bow down to you. Actually, no promises on that one. Good luck.

Fifteen.
Time Travel
-Memory Madness-

"Do what you love and don't settle. Always, always be honest and sincere; people will appreciate you for it...and ultimately respect you in the end. Work as hard as you can and you'll have no regrets." -Michelle Sullivan

The previous chapter discussed the concept of time. But as we grow older, we start to realize that every experience has an impact on us. Is it possible to actually travel back to those memories?

Of course there are picture albums we can flip through to take us back to the "good times", but we can time travel a different way as well. With that being said, let's move it over to Magic's sister: her name is Music.

Listening to specific melodies from the past allows us to be trapped in a moment where all other sounds become silent and vanish; memories start rushing in like waves raging through our minds. When this happens, our feelings resurrect from the beat of the tune. Our emotions surface with every verse we heard each time that song was played on rotation. We understand how specific moments can control us, as we tend to be spectators in our own world. And, sometimes, it makes all of that more confusing as we are paralyzed by our own harmony.

The songs we hear each day return to us and remind us of our lives when we listened to those songs; they define a specific time period for us. Together, the melody, the rhythm, and the beat to a song have the ability to flash memories. These components can bring people back to a specific feeling they might not have felt in a long time.

In a few years, when we hear the songs we listen to today, our feelings will wash over us and the time traveling will begin. No matter how much our lives have changed, the song and the memory that's connected to it, will never change. However, sometimes we must decide which is more important: the actual memories or the lessons we learned from those experiences.

Hopefully, this reflection can help you discover where you see yourself now, as well as where you would like to end up. The past, although unchangeable, can remind you where you desire to be, and what lessons you will bring on that journey.

As we time travel, we are drenched in a pool of emotions. Just as music helps us categorize life into an intangible memory album, magic does the same. Their job is to take various elements and put them together to make a final product, which can impact one's emotions at anytime. These specific moments have to reach our heart and transform our experiences into feelings. Therefore, the concept of time traveling is not about complex machinery or multi-variable equations. Rather, time travel is used through one of the most primal forms of expression. To be able to travel back to the past, whenever you feel the urge to, is a powerful ability to have. So what are you waiting for? Press the Play button, close your eyes, and let your mind drift away.

Name of Effect: "Memory Madness"
Beginner Card Trick

Basic Effect: The performer can memorize the order of a shuffled deck.

What the Audience Sees: The performer has an audience member shuffle the deck. Afterwards, he takes the deck back and tells the audience he can memorize the order of the cards in five seconds. As the audience starts counting, he fans the deck to himself and memorizes the position of all fifty-two cards. Afterwards, he can successfully name each card before dealing it out.

Background: Although this is a beginner trick, this can have a strong impact on hecklers and disbelievers. If you build up your presentation to seem like you memorized all the cards (spoiler alert), then this routine can look incredible.

Method: After the audience hands you the shuffled deck, ask them to count to five as you look through the deck and try to memorize it. As you look through the deck, make sure no one else can see the faces.

While the audience thinks you are memorizing ALL of the cards in the deck, you are only memorizing the bottom card. After the time is up, tell the audience you have successfully memorized every card in the deck and their position.

Once you've memorized the bottom card, place the deck behind your back so no one can see it. While the deck is behind your back, flip the top card over so its face up. Then, bring the deck back out from behind your back and show the audience the bottom of the deck. As you show them the bottom of the deck, name the bottom card aloud (the card you memorized in the beginning).

When you show the audience the bottom of the deck, hold the deck at chest level (vertically), so the audience can ONLY see the bottom card, but you cannot. If done correctly, you'll notice that you can see the top card you just flipped over behind your back, but the audience cannot. Once you've revealed the bottom card to the audience, secretly memorize the top card you flipped face up (the card facing you), and bring the deck behind your back again.

While you bring the deck behind your back for the second time, take the card you just memorized (the top card that was face up) and move this card to the bottom of the deck. Then, flip over the new top card so its face up.

You will then bring out the deck again. As a result, the card you just memorized is facing the audience. This time, name THAT card (the first top card you JUST memorized), and at the same time, note what the new top card is (which is face up facing you). Repeat this process until they believe you memorized the deck.

Let's sum it up:

1. Have someone shuffle the deck.

2. Tell your audience you will memorize the order of the deck within five seconds.

3. Only memorize the bottom card, but fan through the deck as if you're actually memorizing all of the cards.

4. Bring the deck behind your back and flip over the top card so its face up.

5. Take the deck out from behind your back, show the audience the bottom card (so you can't see it), and name the card you noted in the beginning (the bottom card facing the audience).

6. After you name this card aloud, note what the top card is because it should be face up, facing only you.

7. Put the deck back behind your back again and bring the top card you just memorized to the bottom of the deck.

8. Flip over the new top card so its face up.

9. Bring the deck back out from behind your back and show the audience the new bottom card, as you name it (which was the original top card).

10. After you name this card aloud, memorize the new top card that should be facing you (then repeat steps 4-10 until you reach their chosen number).

Presentation Ideas/Alternate Methods/Tips:

"Hi Matt, please mix these cards up as much as you want. That's perfect. Matt, did you know our subconscious notices things faster

than our memory? Therefore, when we perceive many things at once, although we may not memorize it, our subconscious does. Let's try an experiment.

"I'm going to look through the entire deck for exactly five seconds. After five seconds, I'll see if my subconscious noticed the positions of each card in the deck (have the audience count down from five while you look through the deck by yourself acting as if you're "memorizing" every position of every card. Remember to ONLY memorize the bottom card).

"Okay, I think I memorized all of them. I need you to name a number between one and fifty-two. Twenty? Okay, I'll name the first twenty cards in the deck." (Repeat steps 4-10 until you name all twenty cards).

As soon as you name the first card, some people may not be impressed. But as soon as you get past the seventh or eighth card, people will start to really think you memorized the position of every card in the deck.

Also, be careful with angles. When showing the bottom of the deck to the audience, hold the deck naturally at chest level so you can see the top card easily, but people standing next to you cannot. You don't want someone behind you either because they will figure out the whole trick! Good luck.

Sixteen.
Innocence
-Tic-Tac-Toe-

"Family seems to be the most discrete blessing on Earth. You scream, you fight, and you disagree, but you always know they will be there when you get home. To have such a solid factor in this ever-changing life is something to be grateful for." -Angela Wheeler

You're growing old and it's about that time in your life where you know you only have a few years left. Right before death is where your innocence tends to resurface. Looking back at memories, we finally understand we will always be young at heart. This phase in your life is when you want to express your true emotions to the people who are close to you.

Hopefully I don't pass away soon, but just in case anything happens, I want to thank and dedicate this chapter to the four special people who inspire me in everything I do: my siblings.

I was an only child for eleven years until my mother and stepfather got married and had their first child together: Sarah. Words can't describe how wild and crazy she used to be. As I used to wake up from school every morning, attempting to make it to the shower with one eye open, I always saw her on the couch wide awake watching cartoons. Do you know the first thing she would say to me? I would like to hear "Good morning John, how did you sleep?" from a mature seven year old, however I always received "John, I'm hungry. Get me some food."

A few years later they had another child: Jason. Every day when I walked through the front door after school, I saw his eyes glow and smile widen, as he exclaimed, "Bud! Put me on your shoulders!" He couldn't say "John" yet so I guess "Bud" was the next best option.

On the other side of the family, my father and stepmother had twin boys when I was fifteen: Matthew and Jacob. Matthew was the "thinker" and liked to figure things out. Jacob, on the other hand, was the "showman" and embraced life for what it was. At the end of the day (every day), Jacob used to say it was the best day of his life and couldn't wait for tomorrow, but Matthew always wondered why tomorrow was called "tomorrow." They would be a great magic duo.

The innocence I see in my siblings will continuously inspire me. In my eyes, we never really grow up. We just learn how to act in public.

Name of Effect: "Tic-Tac-Toe"
Beginner Miscellaneous Trick

Basic Effect: The performer predicts the outcome of a tic-tac-toe game.

What the Audience Sees: The performer asks an audience member if they want to play a simple game of tic-tac-toe. Once they agree, the performer and the audience member play a casual game, resulting in a tie. The performer admits a tie isn't impressive, however he flips over a napkin revealing that he knew what the outcome would be (and the moves) before the game even started.

Background: This is a neat little routine created by the magician and mathematician Martin Gardner. I highly suggest looking him up because his puzzles and mind magic tricks are unbelievable.

Method: First, create the prediction that is provided (Figure 16.1 Exposed View). Then, flip it over and write down "Prediction" on the back. Put it next to you and don't mention it until the game is over.

Once you're ready to perform, ask your audience member if they want to play a simple game of tic-tac-toe. If they don't try to win, the trick won't work, so make sure they want to win (most people will try to win unless they're hecklers).

Here's the secret move (pun intended): You must perform the first move and it must ALWAYS be in the center square (in this case, the performer will be "X" and the audience will be "O"). Once you've done that, here are the rules for you:

When your audience member **plays a corner**: put your next move in the **open square clockwise** to their move. When your audience member **does not play a corner:** put your next move in the **open square counter-clockwise** to their move.

Once the game is complete, flip over your prediction. If you follow these rules, AND you go first, the results will ALWAYS match the prediction.

Let's sum it up:

1. Draw prediction according to provided picture.

2. Once you start the game, make sure you go in the middle first.

3. Whenever the spectator plays a corner square, put your next move in the square clockwise to their move.

4. If the spectator plays a non-corner square, put your next move in the square counter-clockwise to their move.

5. Once the game is finished, reveal your matching prediction.

Presentation Ideas/Alternate Methods/Tips:

"Hey Tom, do you want to play a game of tic-tac-toe? Great, we can flip a coin to see who goes first; heads I win, tails you lose, ready? Oh boy, it is tails. Okay, I'll go first.

"Hmm...I'm liking the middle, I'll go there first (continue playing the game but remember the rules).

*"Oh man, I guess it was a tie. A tie is pretty impressive, since you **ARE** facing the World Wide Tic-Tac-Toe Champion from 2005. But do you know what's more impressive?" (Flip over your prediction.)*

There are situations where your prediction will not exactly line up with the game. In this case, all you need to do is change the orientation of your prediction when you flip it over. However, you must know what the correct orientation is before flipping it over. You don't want to flip over the prediction and then change the orientation. In other words, flip the prediction over naturally so it should match the actual outcome of your game.

Also, don't mention the prediction beforehand. Just have it next to you and let the audience think you are playing a regular game of tic-tac-toe. In addition, since the trick is a prediction that will work every time, please don't perform this trick twice to the same crowd as they'll realize the outcome will be the same.

Try and think of an easy way to remember the pattern. It will be tough at first, but after looking at the picture a few times, you'll be able to instantly know it off the top of your head when you want to perform.

Have fun taking away the confidence of an elementary school student who just learned how to play tic-tac-toe. Good luck.

O	X	O
O	X	X
X	O	X

Figure 16.1 Exposed View

Left to right:
Matthew, Jason, Jacob, Sarah
October 2012

Seventeen.
Death
-Naked Non-Cents-

"You need to get out there: out in the world and live your life. I can safely say that I have not done this, but I hope to follow my words and experience what life can bring. Life is a funny thing. No one really knows how to interpret it or justify the purpose of what we call 'life'. All I can say is that there is no purpose. It's what you make of it that defines life and everyone will have a different definition." -Brett Powers

As we depart from this world, we finally create our true, and last, definition of what "life" is. This definition is most likely a reflection based off our past experiences and memories.

When looking at a tombstone, most people look at the year you were born and the year you passed away. But what about the line in the middle? In essence, it resembles who you were and what you became. The small line symbolizes the story you told with your existence, only to be passed on by those who were closest to you.

But let's take it a step further. If you knew how and when you were going to die, would you live your life differently? Would you even want this knowledge? Would it change your everyday actions and beliefs?

After those pessimistic questions, what do you do now? Stop reading and go live the life you want to live.

Name of Effect: "Naked Non-Cents"
Advanced Coin Trick

Basic Effect: A coin appears out of thin air.

What the Audience Sees: You are at a pool party with no props and someone asks you to perform a trick. With your hands completely empty and no sleeves, you reach into the air and produce a coin.

Background: First let me tell you that I am no coin magician. Most of my routines involve cards because, in my opinion, you can do a lot more with them.

With that being said, this routine could have already been created for all I know. I wanted to create a visual coin appearance without hiding coins in my hands or special gimmicks...and that could be performed completely naked. What was my inspiration? Well, that's another story.

You can really perform this illusion without any gimmicks, clothing, duplicate coins, tape, magnets, screws, pulleys, rubber bands, or green screens (using a green screen would be pretty cool though). As long as you have an arm and hand, you should be good....in addition to a coin.

Method: Most of you read the description above and probably thought "Hey, so I can just produce money whenever I want?" Well, to the audience it seems that way. But first you need to actually get the money, and then you can perform it. Actually, it doesn't need to be a coin! The object needs to be small enough that it can fit into your armpit, hidden by the width of your forearm. However, the bigger the object, the harder it will be (Figure 17.1 Exposed View).

If you have a shirt on, place the coin on the *outside* of your shirt. Once you've done that, you're ready to perform because that's all the preparation! Now what's the tricky part? To produce the coin. I would recommend practicing in front of a mirror when you read this so you can follow along. This is definitely one of the most angle sensitive illusions in this book, but if done correctly...oh man it is be-a-u-ti-ful.

So you have the coin in your armpit right now, correct? Put your arms straight down to your side near your hips to make sure you look natural. If you move your shoulder and upper body outwards, the coin should fall straight into your hand and it will be concealed by your forearm (Figure 17.2 Exposed View).

Let's sum it up:

1. Place the coin in your armpit.

2. Show your hands are empty and roll up your sleeves.

3. Secretly drop the coin in your hand.

4. Reveal the coin in a creative way.

Presentation Ideas/Alternate Methods/Tips:

Depending on your way of presenting the coin, you can correlate this to the way your arm will move. When you perform this you MUST roll up your sleeves or perform with no sleeves. The method is supporting the idea of no sleeves (hence the name of the trick) because most people will think the coin is in your sleeve if you're wearing sleeves (this is why you can perform this naked!). What if you saw a person who was completely naked making money appear out of nowhere? That would be quite a sight to see!

Before you perform the trick, emphasize to the spectators that you have no sleeves. Also, make sure you show them that you having nothing attached to your waist or clothing. Some people may think you could somehow have a coin attached to your waistline or even hiding something at the end of your shirt near your waist. Just do whatever you can to convince your audience you have no access to a coin.

Let's say you don't have time to prep the coin and place it in your armpit. As long as you have a coin in your pocket, you'll be just fine. The way I travel the coin from my pocket to my armpit is through the actual presentation. For instance, I will ask if they want to see a trick. Hoping they say yes, I put my hands into my pocket. As I do this, I grab the coin and place it into my fist while my hands are in my

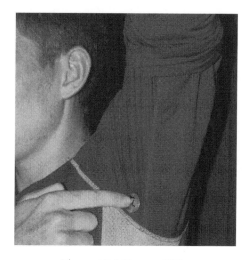

Figure 17.1 Exposed View

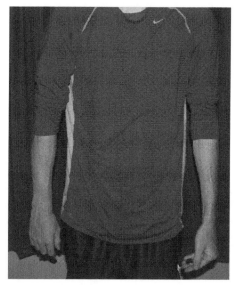

Figure 17.2 Exposed View

pockets. I then explain to the audience there is nothing in my pocket and I show my pockets empty (at this point, the coin is hidden in my hand). I then explain that most magicians hide things in their sleeves so I roll up my sleeves as well. While I roll up my sleeves, I place the coin in my armpit. It doesn't matter what sleeve you roll up first, just make sure that whatever hand you're going to catch the coin with, the opposite hand has the coin and puts it in the correct armpit (the side that will catch the coin). For example, if you want to catch the coin with your right hand, place the coin in your left pocket. This makes it easier because when you roll up your right sleeve with your left hand, you will place the coin in the correct armpit.

One last tip: Never tell the audience what you're going to do before you do it because they will be looking for the coin beforehand. But if you accidentally drop the coin on the floor and don't catch it, your audience members will be confused. At this point, just run away to add more confusion! Good luck.

Eighteen.
Unity
-Colors-

"Life can seem quick. Many people allow themselves to move quickly, thinking they are helping out. For this reason, they miss the simple pleasures and often misdirect the importance of events." –Scott Hutchison

It's a bit ironic that unity results when we lose someone. We start to understand how much this one person impacted us as they connected family and friends who might have never communicated otherwise.

Often times we wonder where a person goes after they die. Most of us glance up in the sky and become curious if there is another "world" out there or not. Of course a death can unite people, but the sky itself can actually bring others together as well. For instance, during the day, we watch the sun slowly wake up, reveal his arrival to the world, and finally say his goodbyes while his colors fuse together. Many people believe this masterpiece is perfection itself; however, it is how this artwork can make us pause what we're doing, look towards the horizon, and come together as a society in the late afternoon and early evening, which creates the real perfection. This inspirational, romantic fire that brightens up the sky ironically becomes more beautiful as it dies. The last look of the sun makes us appreciate it's true value, just like the passing of a person.

As the sun exits, the moon and stars step on stage, yet their show creates more curiosity. We live in a beautiful galaxy with stars lighting up the sky. If stars always die off, then in the far future, what will life be like in empty space? Therefore, if you believe the universe lasts forever, then there are an infinite amount of possibilities. If this happens, then everything you think can't happen now, will happen eventually, right? But if it will happen eventually, do you think you have the ability to make it happen now?

It seems it is in our isolation that we come to know, to understand how we distinguish ourselves from others. We need time away from chaos, family, and society if we ever desire to find that clarity to the best forward movement. When we feel the most alone, most abandoned, the simple forms of attraction remind us of the true beauty in life. Yet, if the sky unites people, then why sometimes when we look at it, do we feel more alone?

The illusion of isolation is misleading because it proves that the real importance of life is simply that we're making it alone, and yet mysteriously together. Enjoy the ride.

Name of Effect: "Colors"
Intermediate Card Trick

Basic Effect: The audience divides the deck into red and black cards without even looking at the face of the cards.

What the Audience Sees: After the deck has been shuffled by the audience, the performer takes the deck back. The performer holds up a card face down and asks an audience member if he or she thinks the card is black (clubs or spades) or red (hearts or diamonds). Under impossible conditions, the spectator guesses every card correctly.

Background: When the audience believes they controlled the outcome of a trick, then it has to be a great effect. This routine has been altered so many times, but the result is the same: the audience mentally knows if the cards are red or black.

Method: For the preparation, separate the deck into all red cards and all black cards (Figure 18.1 Exposed View). Next, ask two people to be the spectators. Look through the deck face up (so only you can see the cards) and divide it where the black and red cards separate. Hand the black half to one spectator and the red half to the other spectator. Then, ask them to shuffle their piles face down so no one can see the location of any cards (this reason also helps to not expose the color of the cards).

Take one pile back and place it on the table face down. Ask for the other pile and place it on top of the first pile. From the audience member's point of view, it seemed they shuffled up half the deck and now you're just putting them back together. Yes, they did that, however they were just mixing up the red cards and black cards, respectively.

Once you have the "shuffled" deck, look through the deck again (so only you can see the cards) and take out one black card and one red card. It doesn't matter what cards they are, as long as the cards are different colors. You could even have audience members name them to make it random.

Place both cards on the table face up next to each other horizontally. These cards will represent the color black and the color red (Figure 18.2 Audience View). Tell your audience you're going to test their psychic ability. If the audience members think the color of the top card is black, you will put the card face down underneath the black card that is already on the table. If the audience members think the color of the top card is red, you will put the card face down underneath the red card that is already on the table. Remember that the audience will only be seeing the back of the card, and they are guessing what color each card is. From their point of view, it's a pretty simple concept.

And how the heck are *you* going to pull this off? You're going to look at the top card before you put it down. Hold the top card so YOU can see the correct color, but the AUDIENCE cannot. No matter WHAT the color of the card is, place the card FACE DOWN under the corresponding pile the AUDIENCE SAYS. As you do this, you will start to realize that you'll just be putting down ALL black cards or ALL red cards (depends which half you collect first from the audience member).

Once you deal out half the deck, you'll realize you're only holding JUST the black cards or JUST the red cards because when you look at the top card, it will be a different color from the color you were

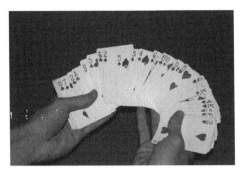

Figure 18.1 Exposed View

Figure 18.2 Audience View

Figure 18.3 Exposed View

just dealing (Figure 18.3 Exposed View). When this happens, pause for a moment and tell your audience that you want to switch things up a little. Take the next card (which should be the opposite colored card of what you were previously dealing) and place it FACE UP on the opposite colored pile. Then, whatever colored pile you were just dealing out, go to that colored pile on the table and flip over any card.

Congratulate your audience on guessing the color correctly and take the card and place it FACE UP on the opposite pile. Tell your audience that these face up cards will represent each color now instead of the face up cards that had previously represented the color (Figure 18.4 Audience View). Hand the deck to one of the audience members and ask THEM to deal out the cards now. However, tell your audience to NOT look at the cards before they deal them out as opposed to what you did. Whatever color they believe the card is, have them start a face down pile underneath the NEW cards that represent each color, just like you did last time. Let the audience deal out the rest of the cards in the deck (Figure 18.5 Audience View).

Once they're finished, you will finally show the results of their psychic ability. Before you show the results, remember that one pile is 100% correct whereas the other pile is 100% incorrect. You need to turn over the INCORRECT pile first, but there's a technique:

First, take ALL of the cards underneath the first face up "representative" card EXCEPT for the "representative" card (Figure 18.6 Audience View). As you pick them up, flip them over in your hand (Figure 18.7 Audience/Exposed View). Then, fan the cards face up underneath the first face-up representative card. Your audience members will not realize that what you just did was a "secret move" (Figure 18.8 Audience View).

With the next pile, take your hands away and have the AUDIENCE flip the cards face up. From the audience's point of view, they guessed all of the colors correctly (Figure 18.9 Audience View).

Figure 18.4 Audience View

Figure 18.5 Audience View

Figure 18.6 Audience View

Figure 18.7 Audience/Exposed View

Figure 18.8 Audience View

Figure 18.9 Audience View

Let's sum it up:

1. Secretly separate the deck into red and black cards before you begin the trick.

2. Split the deck in half (all red, all black) and ask two audience members to shuffle each half individually face down.

3. Bring both halves back together and look at the cards (make sure no one else sees them).

4. Take out one black card and one red card to be the "representatives" of each color and place them on the table horizontally face up. You can have the spectator name two different colored cards if you want.

5. Tell your audience you will test their psychic ability.

6. Take the top card, look at it (make sure you're the only person who sees it) and ask them what color they think it is.

7. No matter what the true color of the card is, place the card face down underneath the "representative" color card of what the audience decided.

8. Continue this process until the color of the top card switches (remember that you will be dealing out one color. Additionally, this process will happen fast because the audience members will start naming random colors).

9. Once the color of the top card changes, tell your audience you want to switch things up.

10. Take that card and place it face UP on the face down pile of the OPPOSITE colored "representative card."

11. Take any face down card from the opposite pile and place this card face UP on the opposite colored "representative card."

12. Hand the deck to the spectator and have him or her deal out the rest of the cards face down in the correct colored pile they think the top card is under the new "representative cards" (make sure they don't look at the card before they deal it out).

13. Once they are done, take the face down cards that are 100% incorrect underneath the first "representative" card, gather them all in your hand in one pile, flip it over, and then spread the pile face up underneath the "representative card."

14. Back up and let your audience flip over the 100% correct pile.

15. Prepare yourself for loud screams.

Presentation Ideas/Alternate Methods/Tips:

Once you perform this trick a few times, the setup won't take long at all. You can actually set it up with a brand new deck of playing cards. If you do a correct riffle shuffle, 95% of the cards will convert to all red and all black. Also, you want the audience to believe that they had full control. Some people will take this so seriously that they will convince their friends they have ESP! Good luck.

Nineteen.
Remembrance
-Under the Hat-

"Live every day with a purpose and a positive attitude. Think about what you want to achieve tomorrow and start it today." –Gregg Wheeler

How do you want to be remembered? At your funeral, who will be there? What will they say about you? Most likely your close family and friends will be there saying positive things, but how long will your story be told until it fades like the end of a love song? I know it's a pretty depressing statement, but in the vast universe, your body resembles one particle of sand, right?

The majority of us don't deserve a statue or proclamation because the people who truly deserve those things have made it possible for us to do our own acts at a free price. You shouldn't get discouraged though because the minor events that you and I perform every day build up to the larger events we witness in the history books. Therefore, all we can do is smile at those symbolic names we read about, realizing they would be nothing without us and we would be nothing without them.

Even though we are all just considered particles of sand in the vast universe, the people who *are* remembered throughout time fall into this category as well. What does this mean? If they can make a difference, why can't you?

Name of Effect: "Under the Hat"
Beginner Bar Trick

Basic Effect: You tell a spectator that you can consume a drink while it sits under a hat without touching the hat.

What the Audience Sees: A drink is poured into a glass and a baseball hat is borrowed. The drink is placed down on the table while the hat is placed over it, covering the drink. The performer bets the audience money that he can drink the drink without lifting up or touching the hat. Of course, the audience doesn't believe him. The performer then puts his head underneath the table for a few seconds and comes up stating some of the drink is gone. The audience is in for a big surprise!

Background: This is a GREAT trick to use at any type of party setting. It fooled me and it's a great way to get free drinks!

Method: If you want to make money (or get free drinks), I suggest you perform this....a lot. First, you need some fishing line, a two-sided mirror, a magnet, and a pancake with chocolate chips. Once you collected those items, measure out two inches on the pancake and tie the fishing line through. Make sure the fishing line doesn't go through any of the chocolate chips or you're in trouble. Next, take the two sided mirror and place it exactly nine and half feet from the table you're performing at. The mirror has to be at least 15 pounds. The magnet? Place it in your pants.

Okay, not really, that was a joke. For the readers who stayed with me and didn't skip this chapter after reading the above paragraph: The real secret? Absolutely nothing. Once you lift your head up from the table, tell the audience that part of the drink is gone and they should lift up the hat to check. Immediately after they lift up the hat, quickly grab the drink and enjoy! In other words, the AUDIENCE does the work for you.

Many of you might be confused on what the "trick" is. Honestly, it's not a magic trick. This is a fun gag you can pull on your friends, family, or even strangers that have a lot of money!

Let's sum it up:

1. Pour yourself a drink and borrow a hat to place over the drink.

2. Bet your audience "something" that you can drink the drink from the hat without touching the hat.

3. Put your head underneath the table and come back up after five seconds. Tell your audience that some of the drink is gone.

4. In disbelief, they will lift up the hat and that's your time to quickly grab the drink and take a sip.

5. Enjoy whatever you bet.

Presentation/Alternative Methods/Tips:

"Hey you. Do you like to gamble? I have a glass with some Coca-Cola in it. Can I borrow your hat? I'll take my drink and put it on the table like this. I'll take your hat and place it over the drink. Is there any possible way I can get to the drink without touching the hat? No? Good.

"I will bet you $1 that I can make some of the Coca-Cola vanish without touching the hat. If I can do this, then you have to give me $1. If I can't do this, then I owe you $1. Deal? (Put your head underneath the table and make some funny noises)

"Okay, some of the Coca-Cola is gone. Don't believe me? Check for yourself! (At this point they will lift up the hat. As soon as they lift up the hat, quickly grab the drink and take a sip).
Oh man, I was thirsty. Thanks!"

Trust me when I say you can have a lot of fun with this one.
Good luck.

Twenty.
Inspiration
-The Newspaper Prediction-

"A lot of you are probably stressed out or unhappy right now. There are things out of our control causing unease every day--natural disasters, threats of violence, etc. But there are a lot of things in our control as well; unfortunately, we're not being really great stewards of those things. Plain and simple: the System is Broken. It takes higher and higher levels of education to be seen as a viable fit to enter the workforce, even though a deep knowledge of 16th Century French Art isn't going to make you a more qualified peanut counter. The ramifications of our dependences on fossil fuels are seen left and right. Our children become more and more likely to be obese, contract diseases and/or experience divorce in their families. Like I said, the system is broken, but WE can fix the system. These are big issues that can be repealed and resolved by making conscientious, small changes to our daily rhythms. It's really just about taking a little extra time. In an era where technology accelerates things more and more for us, we should be looking for the extra time in our days. How badly do you need to drive to the store? Or can you take an extra hour and walk? Can you drive past the fast food drive and into your local grocery store to grab fresh produce instead of French Fries? If you are hiring a manager at your company, can you take five minutes to look beyond the academic credentials on a resume and actually pick up the phone and talk to someone to see if they can contribute to your business? These are all small examples, and I in no way mean to isolate these issues and situations as a means of placing blame. The intent here is to show you--to show everyone--that we CAN make changes to institutions and issues that cause us grief, pain and frustration in our daily lives. I don't need to tell you that the system is broken-you can see it all around you. But I do hope you'll hear me

when I say to you: each and every one of us--no matter how small, how big, how rich or how poor--each of us can contribute to correcting the system. Will you join me in doing so?" -Andrew Stinger

At the end of *your* life, would *you* like to be considered an inspiration? We are constantly encouraged to *search* for inspiration, rather how can we inspire others instead? How can we push family members, friends, and even strangers to reach higher goals and achieve more than what they expected at first? We continuously say we want to, but there is one thing that ***always*** holds us back: the fear of rejection.

Not acting like yourself in fear of being judged is an unfortunate character trait that many of us can relate to. For instance, many people nowadays tend to avoid stepping out of the box, or their comfort zone. This is understandable, for the simple fact that being comfortable with yourself is an important factor in life. However, sometimes it's also acceptable to think from a different point of view in terms of society's "norms." If you do this correctly, you can enjoy life in unique ways that you wouldn't have experienced otherwise. Every once in awhile, take these tips into consideration:

1. You will lose many things in life, but you will always have your imagination.

2. Your talent should not be the only thing people know about you.

3. Love only exists when you let it exist.

4. Society should never determine your true passions.

5. Unpredictable events make life interesting.

6. If you want to innovate, you must learn how to deal with failure.

7. The race for perfection has no finish line.

8. Negative energy in your life is only there to motivate you.

9. If you make a habit to take a new risk every day, you have the potential to change the world.

10. Self-confidence can either make or break your future.

11. In order to be successful, simply live the life you want to live.

12. Don't let society define you.

13. Napping is one of the best things you can do in life.

14. Time is the perfect thief- enjoy what you have while you have it.

15. If you ever want to visit the past again, remember that your memories make up your own personal time machine.

16. Let the youth make you realize how fragile life is, especially since you were once that young.

17. A death in the community should heighten your self-awareness.

18. Since life's journey has an unknown destination, enjoy the ride while you can.

19. One day, you will only be a memory (why not be a good one?)

20. Just be you and see where it goes. Stop worrying. Worrying leads to inaction. Inaction leads to regrets.

Remember you are *always* being judged. If you ever step out of the box, realize that some may think you're a lunatic while others may think you're an inspiration based on their perception of you; it's your job to correctly unite the two. Why? Because the people who do this have true passion, courage, and motivation. In the end, these people are the ones who end up changing the world.

Name of Effect: "The Newspaper Prediction"
Intermediate Mind Trick

Basic Effect: The performer predicts a random line the audience chooses from a newspaper.

What the Audience Sees: An audience member cuts a slice of a column filled with words from a newspaper. The performer looks at the column and writes down a prediction in which no one else sees. Then the performer holds the piece vertically in his hand and uses his other hand to move open scissors up and down the piece of paper. When the audience member freely calls out "stop," the performer immediately cuts the paper. The spectator looks at the section the performer cut (the spot at which the audience said "stop") and it matches the performer's prediction!

Background: Newspaper predictions have always been a huge hit in the world of magic. With that being said, this routine can be performed anywhere, anytime. However, it's perfect for a stage show and it really freaks people out.

Method: Borrow a newspaper or bring your own to perform with. Ask your audience member to pick a page that has no pictures and lots of words (the font should be small). Next, cut out a smaller section from that page so the piece is about 12 inches long vertically by about 2 inches in width. However, make sure there is a full line (or sentence) at the top (make sure you don't cut in the middle of a line). Right now you should have a long strip of newspaper filled with words chosen at random by the audience (Figure 20.1 Audience View).

Next, explain to your audience you will make a prediction. All you need to write down is the top line that you didn't cut through (Figure 20.2 Exposed View). However, don't immediately write it down. You want the audience to think this is completely random, so pretend to look at the newspaper for a few seconds as you "sense" where they will stay stop.

Figure 20.1 Audience View

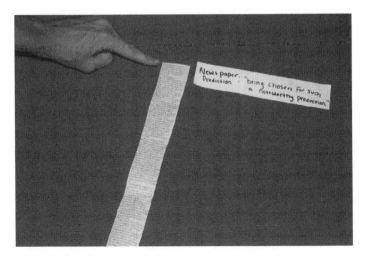

Figure 20.2 Exposed View

After a few seconds of acting, you can put the column down, write your prediction, and then flip over the prediction so no one can read it (Figure 20.3 Audience View).

And here comes my favorite part of the trick: as you hold the column vertically to your audience, just hold the column upside down! This means that the top line, the one you wrote down, should be at the bottom towards the floor. If the font is small enough and you're at least three feet away from the audience, they won't even notice!

With your other hand, prepare the scissors and move them up and down the column. Have an audience member call stop whenever he or she wants, and cut the newspaper at that exact spot. Just make sure it's a straight line (Figure 20.4 Audience View). After you cut the piece, the bottom half will flutter to the ground, meaning you are in the home stretch. Tell the audience you don't want to touch the piece just in case they think you will somehow switch the paper.

Have a person read the line at which they called "stop" then flip over your prediction. The audience will believe that the line they are reading is from the spot they said "stop" because they don't know you were holding the column upside down! (Figure 20.5 Audience View).

Let's sum it up:

1. Borrow a piece of newspaper.

2. Have an audience member select a section where there are lots of small words and no pictures.

3. Cut out that section, but make sure you can read the top line.

4. Tell your audience that you will make a prediction based on the article they selected.

5. Read the top line, remember it, and skim the rest of the article for about five seconds.

6. Write down your prediction (the top line) and flip it over so no one can see it.

Figure 20.3 Audience View

Figure 20.4 Audience View

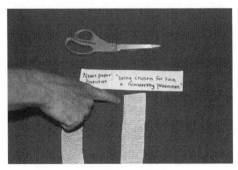

Figure 20.5 Audience View

7. Stand a few feet away from the audience and hold the piece of paper in one hand vertically, but upside down.

8. With your other hand, use scissors to go up and down the column vertically and have an audience member call out "stop."

9. When he or she says "stop," stop moving the scissors and cut the piece in a straight line.

10. The bottom half of the paper will fall to the floor.

11. Have an audience member pick it up, read the line, and flip over your prediction.

12. Get the tissues out because people will start to cry over how amazing you are.

Presentation Ideas/Alternate Methods/Tips:

"Jude, can you come on stage for me? Great.

"As you can see, I have today's newspaper. If you could choose any section with lots of small words and no pictures, that would be perfect.

"I'll cut out that section just for you (make sure you cut a spot where you can read the top line. However, it doesn't have to be the very first line of the article they select). Now since you made a random selection, I'm going to make a random prediction. First, let me read the article. Hmm...hmm...pretty interesting stuff here (just read what the top line is and act as if you're skimming the article). Okay, I think I have a prediction. I'll write it down on the whiteboard.

"With one hand I'll hold the article vertically and with my other hand I'll go up and down with the scissors (hold article upside down). Whenever you feel the urge for me to stop, just call out 'Stop!' as I go up and down. Right there? Okay, I'm cutting it!

"As you can see the piece fell to the ground. Can you pick it up for me so you don't think I switched anything? Please read aloud the line that you stopped at. As you do that, I'll flip over my prediction."

This routine can get a huge reaction with the correct presentation. However, in the performance, make sure the audience believes everything is random. One suggestion is to use a long strip of paper. In this case, there's more of an opportunity for the audience member to call out "Stop!" when they want. When you cut the section, try to have the top line in the middle or the end of a sentence as this will be more random. If the top line is the beginning of the article (or the beginning of a sentence) it may be a tad awkward as it might reveal the method because this is also your prediction.

Also, make sure the piece looks similar when you flip it upside down. Obviously you will realize it's upside down, but the audience won't even notice. A good way to prevent this is to use an article with small font. In addition, you need to make sure when the audience member calls out "stop," you cut it STRAIGHT. If you don't, the audience will read where they actually called out "stop" and that wouldn't be good! Good luck.

The Finale

The Perfect Illusion.

Hopefully it is evident that life can be considered an illusion since new discoveries are constantly creating new ideas and redefining reality for us. As a result, it's not what you look at that matters, but it's how you see it. If we look at things from a different angle sometimes, we start to realize that not everything we perceive is the absolute truth. Not just with magic, but with life in general.

Remember: one reason why people give up so fast on their goals is because they tend to look at how far they **still** have to travel, rather than how far they have **already** traveled. The difference between those who succeed and those who fail is how they deal with the obstacles they encounter. Many people exaggerate the small obstacles, using these "barriers" as rational excuses for their failures. If you want to avoid this mindset, you must use these obstacles and failures as great opportunities to modify and strengthen your skills. Ultimately, you use these skills to achieve what you have been chasing all along.

You cannot control every aspect in your life. But you DO have control of how you perceive each situation and your response to it. It's the power of your choices and attitudes that will impact your perception of each situation. If done correctly, you can also determine your happiness and success. Now, go out there and make it your best day ever. Why? More importantly, why not?

But where did it all start? With a magic trick. The art of magic challenges the assumptions people have about what can and cannot be accomplished. It's not about the tricks, but their impact on people.

For instance, a magic trick can alter our views and question if life is really the way we perceive it to be. In other words, one simple magic trick can change the way we think. If we start to think differently, we can create new potential for ourselves to make a difference in the world. So the next time you perceive something and don't know if it's true or not, enjoy it; it's for your own good. Our reality is influenced by our own ideas about reality, in spite of the true nature behind these ideas we create for ourselves.

It doesn't have to be about tricks, as long as your audience changes their perspective on a specific matter. You need to add something to your presentation so people are not only impressed, but motivated. Not only motivated, but inspired. Not only inspired, but encouraged to take action into the lives of others, including their own. This can be done by looking at situations from a different angle.

We create visions for our own future whether we realize it or not. However, when something does not match our expectations, we naturally question how it occurred and shut down when it doesn't make sense. But that's the best part about the art of magic: this confusion transforms into amazement, wonder, and curiosity because the more you think you see something, the easier it is to get fooled.

When we entered this world, we knew nothing as our environment created who we became and taught us our own reality. If we start to think about something more, and practice it more, we tend to believe it more. The things we focus on, practice, and engage continue to shape us. When I perform, I try to break that boundary between what society has trained us to see and our true authentic imagination. As you watch a magic trick, somewhere, deep down in your heart, you want it to be true. But as you witness it, you tell yourself it's humanly impossible to do, so you disregard your faith and automatically believe it's not real. That little spot in your heart where you want it to be real, and you know it's not, creates disappointment from being taught the worst lesson of all: not to believe.

I may not be who you think I am. You may not be who you think you are. We only compare ourselves to other people, taking traits and characteristics from the ones we admire and learning from the ones we don't. We base these beliefs and thoughts on our environment and experiences as we as we constantly compare and critique everything and everyone in our environment. This is how society has formed us. I'm not saying it's wrong. I'm not saying it's right. I'm just saying that's how it is.

Throughout life people have been taught that certain hopes and desires can't be achieved, but magic defeats this concept. At a young age, we believe we can accomplish anything we want with no buffer between our dreams and realities. However, when we grow, we lose this perception. We lose this belief. We lose one of the most important traits a human being can ever possess: our imagination.

When I travel and meet new people with different backgrounds and views, the differences they individually have don't matter at the moment. Why? Because after I perform, they all have one thing in common: witnessing the concept of impossibility shatter. As a result, this creates enjoyment and excitement. For a moment, we believe miracles are possible. For a moment, we believe magic could be real. For a moment, we believe the boundary between reality and imagination has been broken.

When this boundary becomes broken, it creates a special memory for people to add to their "time machines." We can't control these machines, but we can create the quality of them, as we try to generate positive memories that we can travel to at any time. Even if people don't remember who I am, they can look back on their lives and remember that specific moment when they witnessed "magic." They will remember that specific moment when they experienced the impossible become possible. They will remember that specific moment and smile. If you can make at least one person smile using anything you learned from this book, then I have done my job.

Your experiences will always become richer. Your knowledge will continuously grow. But guess what? Life goes on. It's what you do with these gifts that define you: The world is your stage. Life is your show. *Go and perform.*

Is magic real? It's what you want to believe. Most people think of magic as performing "tricks." Yet, real magic lies within us. That's the thing with magic: it's always here. How? Well, magic is traveling back in time and realizing the changes you went through to create who you have become at this very moment: the decisions you made, the friends you gained, and the memories you possess. Sometimes society will try and alter who you are and convince you that some of your goals in life are impossible to achieve. This is when you have to learn that "impossible" is just a word and you can't let society use this word to control your happiness. Personally, achieving your goals and creating happiness for yourself and others in spite of your worries is real magic.

We have to realize that society creates our own illusions, roots them in our brains, and they soon act as a replacement for understanding issues and being accepted. These individual illusions soon build up to create what we refer to as "life." And when these illusions work well enough, they are passed on to the next generation. However, the fact that society has trained us to believe in these, my dear reader, is the *perfect illusion.*

Final Thoughts.

We must leave each other at some moment or another. I know, I know, it's a gloomy feeling, but everyone can relate to that sense of sadness and achievement as the last chapter of a book is read.

It's easy for performers to be frustrated because we have to battle each day between what the world is and what we can actually make of it. I guess we try as hard as we can, yet we can never change every person's perspective. I know that I'll keep trying, but will you?

Performers gather people together that would never communicate otherwise. Whenever you gather a crowd that is focused on something other than themselves and their differences, with no negative energy involved, there is a beautiful connection. Watching people come together and be amazed at the same time is more amazing than what caused them to be amazed in the first place.

The only "magic" I *really* perform is dissolving the walls we create within ourselves to separate us from others. The wonder people experience creates the only thing remaining: unity. Magic is one of the few things in life that lets this idea become possible. When you're touched by this art, nothing in the world is ever quite the same.

Let's go back to the first page of this book. It introduced a dream which I haven't brought up since the beginning. This time please read it more carefully. You can try to analyze it as much as you want, but more importantly, try to imagine the situation actually happening to you.

Imagine the spotlight in your face. You can feel the heat from the shine. You're on stage. It seems like a normal stage, but it's not-trust me.

You turn around and see a person behind you waiting their turn. You see a person behind him. Then another person behind her. And so on.

These strangers waiting in line are filled with their own knowledge, insight, and advice. They come from many different backgrounds, cultures, and beliefs. They are young and old. They are rich and poor. They are ambitious and content.

You realize this is it.
There is no turning back.
No second chances.
The entire human race is staring at you.
And you have one chance to say one thing.

It could be a word. It could be a sentence. It could be a paragraph. It could be anything. Anything at all.

Before you, others have spoken words of wisdom. These voices will still echo after your turn. Now is when you must decide whether or not your voice will echo as loudly, or if it will be a faint whisper that disappears quietly.

As you stand there silently for a moment on stage, your eyes gaze the crowd. You see the young and the old. You see the rich and the poor. You see the ambitious and the content.

These differences only inspire you. This inspiration helps you rear-range your thoughts as you finally realize what you will say.

You take a deep breath, reach for the microphone, and just as you're about to start speaking...

Now that you've read the dream again, write down your own answer with honesty, sincerity, and originality. If you're comfortable sharing your response, you may send it to me once it is finished. Believe it or not, even if I don't know you, I'm still curious in what you would say if you were given this rare opportunity in front of so many people (please take as long as possible).

Before you write anything down, just remember this: When you're in a big crowd you might want to say something inspirational, powerful, or memorable. However, sometimes it's not what you truly believe because you only have one chance to reveal your exact views and beliefs. Therefore, you could rush your thoughts and it may be hard to express your true emotions.

Everyone has their own story. We each have a unique perspective of what life is, yet we must not forget to accept that others have their own perspective as well. Next time you walk by someone in a store or down the street, understand that each random passerby has their own authentic life as you do. It is characterized by their own routines, goals, and anxieties, yet they are invisible to you. All you see is their appearance on the outside, but deep down they have their own internal and underground complex tunnels that connect to thousands of other lives and memories. When you walk by this person, you will now just be an additional blur to the background of their multifaceted experiences. But it's up to you: do you want to be a blur or a vivid memory?

If you were given one chance to say anything to the world, you might talk about family and friends, goals and ambitions, or memories and lessons you've learned throughout your life that could help benefit society. All of those topics are great, they truly are. But do you know what I would say? If I had one chance? If the spotlight was on me? I'll let you decide.

Further Reading Recommendations:

Psychological Subtleties
By Banachek

Modern Coin Magic
By J.B. Bobo

The Alchemist
By Paulo Coehlo

13 Steps to Mentalism
By Corinda

Seven Habits of Highly Effective People
by Stephen R. Covey

The Practical Encyclopedia of Magic
By Nicholas Einhorn

Card College: A Complete Course in Sleight-of-Hand Card Magic
By Roberto Giobbis

Blink
By Malcom Gladwell

Damn Good Advice (for people with talent!)
by George Lois

The Sociological Imagination
By C. Wright Mills

The Last Lecture
By Randy Pausch

Mark Wilson's Complete Course in Magic
By Mark Wilson

The Author:

John Duke Logan (born October 7th, 1993) is an entertainer, author, and entrepreneur from Hanover, Massachusetts. He's been performing the art of magic since he was twelve years old and now travels the country sharing it on stage and close up at a variety of events. In his eyes, magic isn't just an art; it's a tool that can change lives.

---

www.johndukelogan.com

31670523R00100

Made in the USA
Charleston, SC
24 July 2014